MAKE THE BIBLE LIVE

MAKE
THE BIBLE
LIVE

A BASIC GUIDE FOR

PREACHERS AND TEACHERS

by

GLENN O'NEAL

BMH BOOKS
Winona Lake, Indiana 46590

ACKNOWLEDGMENT

It was under the teaching of the late Alva J. McClain while studying at Grace Theological Seminary that I received an exposure to the problem-solution approach to sermon preparation. Some of the ideas presented herein were obtained from the lectures of this able expositor. This would apply especially to the section relating to gathering material from the text. I owe a continuing debt of gratitude to him for his instruction.

TABLE OF CONTENTS

INTRODUCTION

The decline in the influence of the pulpit has become an increasing concern to church leaders. Pulpit committees are asking for pastors who can expound the Word of God. Yet, in spite of a growing number of seminary trained men, the expository type of preacher seems difficult to find. This book is written with the hope that a contribution toward meeting this need will be realized.

Many fine treatises on expository preaching have been published. However, the unique contribution of this book is its explanation of ways to explore the depths of the Word. Also, the methods of sermon development, each of which employs the problem-solution type of outline, should prove helpful. It is my prayer that this book will challenge ministers to renew their efforts to combine the goal of preaching the Word with that of meeting the spiritual needs of people.

It is not my intent to suggest that the preaching method advocated herein is the only legitimate system. Every preacher, however, should be acquainted with the problem-solution approach. Variations are simple when a basic plan such as this is clearly understood.

The material presented should provide a valuable source of help for the seminary student, as well as the pastor, who desires to sharpen his pulpit ministry. The layman seeking ways to discover the truth of the Word and organize it for presentation will find the treatment understandable and challenging.

CHAPTER I

PREREQUISITES FOR A PULPIT MINISTRY

This chapter is designed not only as an introduction to the book, but also as an example of the expository method of preaching and teaching the Word of God which is advocated by the author.

PREREQUISITES FOR A
PULPIT MINISTRY

Pastor Timothy was having problems. Some of the leaders were challenging his teaching and he was impatient with those who were slow to respond to his exhortations. Not everyone was happy with his ministry. Decisions had to be made. Should he deal with the issues firmly? Should he resign? Should he wait for the problem to resolve itself?

When word of the problem reached the Apostle Paul, he carefully penned a letter "to Timothy, my beloved son . . ." (II Timothy 1:2).* Paul's thoughtful counsel to Timothy has been a source of challenge to Gospel ministers ever since.

Both I and II Timothy have provided a solid basis for establishing standards for young men entering the ministry. The book of II Timothy is especially helpful in providing reassurance to the pastor whose confidence has been shaken by problems similar to those of Timothy. Everyone who is called to proclaim the Word of God must carefully establish principles on which his ministry will be based. Paul warns Timothy that many people will not want teachers who possess such standards when he declares, ". . . the time will come when they will not endure sound doctrine; but wanting to have their ears tickled, they will accumulate for themselves teachers in accordance to their own desires" (4:3).† In other words, some people will look for teachers who say only what they want to hear.

This search may take the form of looking for the preacher with the most abundant supply of jokes or the cleverest use of language. It could involve careful scru-

---

*All quotations are from the *New American Standard Bible*.
†All verse references in Chapter I are from II Timothy unless otherwise noted.

tiny of his choice of subject material, shunning the one who would treat topics which are unpopular. The preacher also may be expected not to preach on anything controversial which, in some situations, would drastically limit his choice of material.

It is sometimes comforting to realize that the dilemma of the preacher is not new. Even in Paul's day there were many by-paths beckoning the one who was attempting to proclaim God's message. Timothy was urged by Paul to "retain the standard of sound words which you have heard from me . . ." (1:13a). His reminder to Timothy of these standards should be helpful to every minister in setting his goals for a preaching ministry. They would also prove of benefit to every church as it seeks God's choice for a pulpit minister.

What was the "standard of sound words" to which Paul refers which was a treasure to be guarded (1:14)?

THE MINISTER'S
MANNER OF LIFE

The first standard of which he speaks is the *minister's manner of life*. The exhortation to Timothy was, "you therefore, my son, be strong in the grace that is in Christ Jesus" (2:1). A paraphrase of this verse could be, "let every area of your life demonstrate the strength that comes from the grace of the abiding presence of Christ." Before he counseled him as to what he was to *say*, he dealt with what he was to *be*. The constancy of complaints from the laity emphasize the fact that the need for this exhortation has not diminished.

One church member put it this way, "If our pastor could fly in on Saturday night, preach on Sunday, and then fly out on Monday morning, everything would be wonderful. He's a good speaker, but when you live in the same community with him and his family through the week, you have difficulty listening to his message on Sunday."

SUFFERING HARDSHIP

An important area of strength relating to the minister's manner of life is the *willingness to "suffer hardship"* for the honor of Jesus Christ. Paul invited him to "suffer hardship with me" (2:3) or, in other words, "take your share of the suffering."

This is in contrast to statements commonly heard among ministers and prospective ministers: "He really has an ideal setup in that church," or, "I'm glad to hear he received the advancement. He deserved a call to a larger church."

Three illustrations emphasize the task of the ministry and all speak of the personal sacrifice involved. The soldier only succeeds as he suffers hardship in pleasing the one who enlisted him (2:3, 4). The athlete receives the prize by following the rules laid down by others (2:5). The farmer receives his share of the crops only after working hard (2:6). Paul concludes this exhortation by presenting what should be a continuous challenge to those who would use the ministry for their own purposes: he was willing to "suffer hardship, even imprisonment as a criminal" (2:9), for the honor of the Christ he served.

PERSONAL PURITY

Another necessary characteristic of the minister's manner of life is a *demonstration of personal purity.* The last statement of 2:19 is, ". . . Let every one who names the name of the Lord abstain from wickedness." Paul then compares the servant of the Lord to the pot or pan used in a home and declares that "if a man cleanses himself from these things, he will be a vessel for honor, sanctified, useful to the Master, prepared for every good work" (2:21). The "these things" evidently refers to the aforementioned wickedness which

15

was being perpetrated by the worldly and empty chatter of Hymenaeus and Philetus. Paul stresses the diligence with which one must seek this inner purity and sincere purpose of honoring Christ when he adds, "Now flee from youthful lusts, and pursue after righteousness, faith, love and peace, with those who call on the Lord from a pure heart" (2:22).

The message which the preacher delivers begins long before he enters the pulpit. It starts in the demonstration of words and deeds which his audience has observed. It may come from a good reputation which has been reported by others. However it comes, there is no justification for a minister to expect a favorable response to his message, or to assume his congregation will build a sincere purpose of life, unless he himself has responded wholeheartedly in dedication of his life to Christ.

THE MINISTER'S ATTITUDE
TOWARD PEOPLE

The second "standard of sound words" of which Paul speaks, involves *the minister's attitude toward people.*

A rude awakening for many ministers is the slow response of people to the simple gospel of Jesus Christ, and their hesitancy to grow in the Christian life.

Constantly the minister is faced with discouragements as he attempts to minister to the needs of his flock. Slight differences in minor points of doctrine become the test of whether one Christian will fellowship with another. A divergence of views on some organizational policy sows seeds of division which seem never to be healed.

Timothy was experiencing a conflict over the teaching of a divisive doctrine. There were those who had been spreading the idea ". . . that the resurrection has already taken place, and thus they upset the faith of some" (2:18).

The reaction of a pastor to such problems usually takes one of two forms. The easiest way out is to become discouraged and quit. "I love to preach," he might reason, "but I just can't stand these unstable people!" Another possible response is to exert his authority with severity. "I'm going to clean up this problem if it's the last thing I do." "What this church needs is a good house cleaning!" The trouble with the latter response is that often when the broom has swept clean, he has no one left to listen to him preach, or pay his salary!

LOVING AS CHRIST LOVES

Paul reminds Timothy that a part of being "strong in the grace that is in Christ Jesus" (2:1) is to demonstrate to people the same love that caused Christ to pray for those who were crucifying Him: "Father, forgive them for they do not know what they are doing" (Luke 23:34). Paul's word to Timothy was, "The Lord's bondservant must not be quarrelsome, but be kind to all, able to teach, patient when wronged, with gentleness correcting those who are in opposition . . ." (2:24, 25a). The pastor constantly encounters those who vex his soul because of their selfish opposition to the advancement of the cause of Christ. Not all of these will be outside the church of Christ. The effective minister must develop the attitude of forbearance by constantly reminding himself that every individual is a soul for whom Christ died and thus has value and exciting potential.

Paul left no delusions as to the task before him in dealing with wicked men ensnared by the devil (2:26). He even suggested that "in the last days" these men will be even more intense in their opposition (3:1). Some of the attributes listed were, ". . . lovers of self, lovers of money, boastful, arrogant, revilers, disobedient to parents, ungrateful, unholy, unloving, irreconcilable, malicious gossips, without self-control, brutal, haters of good, treacherous, reckless, conceited, lovers of pleasure rather than lovers of God" (3:2-4).

17

In spite of these discouraging prospects, Paul concludes his exhortation to Timothy by declaring that "I solemnly charge you in the presence of God and of Christ Jesus, who is to judge the living and the dead, . . . preach the Word . . ." (4:1, 2a).

In determining his attitude toward people, the effective preacher should keep constantly in mind that everyone with whom he speaks, no matter how unresponsive, will have to answer to Jesus Christ. This is a sobering thought, and the basis for challenge. The minister is to ". . . be ready in season and out of season; reprove, rebuke, exhort, with great patience and instruction" (4:2).

In spite of the fact that one must look at opposition from the world realistically, a constant encouragement to the minister is the possibility that "God may grant them repentance leading to the knowledge of the truth, and they may come to their senses and escape from the snare of the devil . . ." (2:25, 26). One of the greatest joys that comes to a pastor is to see lives who have been "delivered . . . from the domain of darkness, and transferred . . . to the kingdom of His beloved Son" (Colossians 1:13). If ever the preacher loses the expectation of the transformation of lives, he has lost much of his effectiveness.

In spite of the deceivers there are many who come to the Lord, grow in the faith and constantly demonstrate the reality of the power of God in their lives. These are the ones of whom Paul speaks as he tells Timothy that ". . . the things which you have heard from me in the presence of many witnesses, these entrust to faithful men, who will be able to teach others also" (2:2). To see one's ministry multiplied by the teaching program of those who have responded to the gospel because of his efforts, that is the reward which spurs the pastor to constantly minister to a world that is being ". . . held captive . . ." (2:26).

After serving as a pastor for twenty-five years, it has been my observation that the people who produce joy in the ministry are legion. Even though the foregoing warning in regard to the wicked and deceitful is legitimate, the rewards of observing the responsive causes the miseries produced by those who would oppose the work of Christ to fade into insignificance.

THE MINISTER'S PRESENTATION
OF THE WORD OF GOD

A further "standard of sound words" worthy of consideration is *instruction in relation to the presentation of the Word of God.*

Evidently Timothy was in danger of succumbing to the temptation of minimizing the importance of the forthright proclamation of the Word of God. Perhaps the opposition had caused him to reduce his forcefulness, or the false teachers had lured him into the snare of dealing with side issues. Whatever the problem, Paul exhorted him ". . . to kindle afresh the gift of God which is in you through the laying on of my hands. For God has not given us a spirit of timidity, but of power and love and discipline. Therefore, do not be ashamed of the testimony of our Lord, or of me His prisoner; but join with me in suffering for the gospel according to the power of God" (1:6-8).

Throughout the book Paul constantly challenges Timothy to present God's message with confidence and enthusiasm. Of particular help are his answers to four questions that are vital for an effective ministry of the Word of God.

1. Why should one believe it?

He first of all points out that the basis for boldness in preaching the gospel is the fact that God's eternal plan has been made sure by

". . . the appearing of our Savior Christ Jesus, who abolished death, and brought life and immortality to light through the gospel" (1:10). The appearance of Christ after his death is a substantiation for the claims about Christ recorded in the Old Testament. He chided the doubting disciples by declaring, "O foolish men and slow of heart to believe in *all* that the prophets have spoken!" (Luke 24:25). Luke then affirms that ". . . beginning with Moses and with all the prophets, He explained to them the things concerning Himself in all the Scriptures" (Luke 24:27). Thus the risen Christ places His stamp of approval upon the authority of the Old Testament.

The Bible is constantly under attack. The one who is called to preach the Word of God must be convinced that God has spoken! Paul gives the reassuring affirmation that "all Scripture is inspired by God . . ." (3:16). The preacher's task is to proclaim that revelation.

2. What is the central theme of God's revelation?

The thrust of the apostle's message found in his challenge to "remember Jesus Christ, risen from the dead, descendant of David, according to my gospel" (2:8). Proper occupation with these truths which involve the person of Christ, the purpose of His first coming, and the promise of the second coming, will be a constant deterrent to wrangling about words without purpose (2:14), and engaging in ". . . worldly and empty chatter . . ." (2:16).

It is apparent that the whole Word of God focuses upon this major theme. The preacher's task is to relate faithfully that theme as it is found in the entire Word of God. Paul counsels Timothy to "Be diligent to present yourself approved unto God as a workman who does not need to be ashamed, handling accurately the word of truth" (2:15). The "workman" with which he would be most familiar would be the tentmaker. It is interesting to note that the word "handling accurately" literally means "to cut straight." Now what would cause a tentmaker to be most embarrassed? Probably it would be to have a piece of material fail to fit the pattern because he had not cut it straight. His plea is obvious. Be careful in the treatment of the Word so that all the pieces fit together according to God's plan.

Of course, in order to fit all the pieces together one must dedicate himself to deal with the whole of Scripture in his ministry. Men must be led to see the marvels of how all of revelation relates to the divine pattern.

3. What will be the effect on the hearer?

The first effect will be enlightenment which will lead the hearer to a knowledge of Christ as his Savior. Paul reminds Timothy ". . . that from childhood you have known the sacred writings which are able to give you the wisdom that leads to salvation through faith which is in Christ Jesus" (3:15).

Once a person has responded to the gospel, the Word of God becomes the means by which he is equipped for a productive Christian life (3:17). It is good for "teaching" (3:16) because it is the infallible source of truth. "Reproof" (3:16) probably refers to that which enables one to refute the false teacher but could also involve the ability to resist any suggestion which would lead to looseness of morals. "Correction" (3:16) refers to improvements or revisions of life necessary to put a person on the path of pleasing

God. "Training in righteousness" (3:16) enables one to mature in his dedication to Christ with a growing discernment of His will in every phase of life.

Anyone who has observed a body of believers will recognize that these effects are desperately needed to revitalize the church. The pastor must dedicate himself to preaching the Word if he hopes to accomplish these results.

4. How should one proclaim the Word?

The command is to "preach the Word . . ." (4:2). The usual word emphasis given to this phrase is "Preach the *Word.*" However, there are reasons to believe that the intent was for the word stress to be *"Preach* the Word." This is indicated by the solemnity of the charge given in verse one, and the meaning of the word "preach" which is "to herald a message." Further evidence for this contention is emphasized by the words "be ready in season and out of season" (4:2) which would seemingly refer to the action of preaching.

Most people would agree that there is a dire need for preachers who herald the message with urgency. There are many sincere, dedicated ministers of the gospel, but it is alarming to find that many of them sound like they don't really believe the message they preach. In contrast to the ability of a great actor to make that which is unreal become real, many preachers make what is real seem very unreal. One remedy is for the minister daily to ask the Lord to make the message of God's revelation vitally important; ask Him for a sense of urgency stemming from the high privilege and responsibility he has in proclaiming it; and ask Him for enablement from the Holy Spirit to proclaim the message with life-saving power.

Not only must this message be presented with urgency, but it needs to be proclaimed vividly. Paul didn't say this in his letter to Timothy, but he practiced it. He constantly used enlightening illustrations which made the truth come to life.

Notice several of these vivid illustrations in chapter two, some of which have already been mentioned. He used three pictures to stress the idea of dedication to the task; the soldier (3, 4), the athlete (5), and the farmer (6). He compared the diligence of one who handles the Word of God to a workman who does not want to be embarrassed with his work (15). The word of wicked Hymenaeus and Philetus is referred to as "gangrene" (17). The analogy is made between the honored servant and the honored vessel in a large house (20, 21). He concluded with a reference to the state of the deceived as being "held captive" in "the snare of the devil" (26).

If a preacher would apply himself diligently to the task of developing applicable illustrations, he would find a marked improvement in the attention of the listeners as well as their comprehension of the message. The Lord apparently felt this was a necessity. He constantly spoke of the sower who went to sow, the prodigal son, the ones on whom the tower of Siloam fell, the wedding feast. He presented spiritual truth by employing illustrations from the everyday activities of people. Preachers would do well to take some lessons in this regard from the Master Teacher!

So far we have talked about three standards that are of vital concern to the minister; namely, his *manner of life, his attitude toward people,* and his *presentation of the Word of God.* The Lord we serve, the life-giving message we have to proclaim, and the eternal welfare of the souls for whom we are responsible demand that we not be satisfied with mediocrity. The ministry must be challenged to higher standards.

Again Paul's words to Timothy were, "Retain the standard of sound words which you have heard from me, in the faith and love which are in Christ Jesus. Guard through the Holy Spirit who dwells in us, the treasure which has been entrusted to you" (1:13, 14).

Chapter II

ORGANIZING
THE EXPOSITORY SERMON

ORGANIZING THE EXPOSITORY SERMON

THE GOAL OF PREACHING

The goal of preaching is to communicate the revelation of God, contained in the Word of God, and to relate it to the needs of people. As the minister approaches the pulpit he must recognize that he is an ambassador, that is, one sent as an official representative obligated to speak as instructed by the sender. This truth is emphasized in consecutive verses in II Corinthians five. God "gave us the ministry of reconciliation" (18). "He has committed to us the word of reconciliation" (19). "Therefore, we are ambassadors for Christ, as though God were entreating through us; we beg you on behalf of Christ, be reconciled to God" (20).

Paul reminded Timothy of the means by which he was brought to the place of reconciliation when he stated ". . . that from childhood you have known the *sacred writings* which are able to give you the wisdom that leads to salvation through faith which is in Christ Jesus" (II Timothy 3:15). The "sacred writings" were the content of the teaching. The one who would be a faithful ambassador must likewise make the communication of the truth of those writings the heart of his message.

The goal is twofold. First, God's "word of reconciliation" (19) must be presented. Men are to be told what God has done. But God is *entreating* through us" (20). Paul says "we *beg you* on behalf of Christ" (20). The emphasis of these words would indicate the need for a passionate plea based on a sincere concern for people. This is the second phase of the goal of preaching.

THE CLASSIFICATION OF SERMON TEXTS

The traditional classification of sermons has been textual, topical and expository. The typical textual sermon consists of a thought taken from the Bible. However, frequently there is no intent on the part of the preacher to explain what the Word actually says. Material for the sermon often is gleaned from outside sources, which may include quotations, anecdotes, statistics, and other sources which are available to speakers in general. Often the appeal for action is based on the theme derived from the text rather than the actual message of the passage.

For example, Romans 1:14 might be chosen as a text. It reads, "I am under obligation both to Greeks and to Barbarians, both to the wise and to foolish." The method of development could be to stress the ones to whom we are obligated, with little if any effort being made to indicate the reason Paul wrote it, and the meaning of the actual words. Thus the textual preacher's task often becomes a weekly search for seed thoughts around which he can relate the material gleaned from sources outside the Bible, and still retain a vague feeling of biblical flavor.

The topical sermon can be expository. However, in usual practice this is not the case. Common procedure is to decide on a subject and then search out Bible proof texts to substantiate a series of ideas which relate to the subject. In spite of the fact that many successful preachers have established their hearers in Bible truth in this manner, a major shortcoming is that the texts are often read, but no explanation is offered. Frequently little effort is given to show the relation of the verse to the subject.

The expository sermon in traditional practice could best be described as a running commentary on an extended passage of Scripture. The method is sometimes referred to as a "Bible reading." The listener encounters a problem in this type of sermon. The variety of thoughts are difficult to relate to an overall theme, thus, reducing meaningful impact. The passage of Scripture may be explained but not made vital to the listener.

Assuming that you adopt the previously discussed goal of preaching, namely, the proclaiming of God's message with God's heart for the needs of people, a classification of sermon texts seems unnecessary. If you are heeding the admonition to "preach the word," every sermon should be expository in the sense that it exposes what the Word says. However, it is possible to recognize at least two classifications of texts from the expository viewpoint, namely, the single text, including short and extended passages, and the selected group of passages. In each case the goal would be to present what the Scripture declares. The following are examples of these approaches:

1. THE SINGLE TEXT.

a. The short passage.

"But as many as received Him, to them He gave the right to become children of God, even to those who believe in His name: who were born not of blood, nor of the will of the flesh, nor of the will of man, but of God" (John 1:12-13).

Expository outline: Statement of problem—How can one become a child of God?

I. Responding in the proper manner to Christ, verse 12.

II. Experiencing a work that only God can accomplish, verse 13.

NOTE: The expository method does not depend on the length of the passage. Sometimes a speaker may develop a single statement such as "The Word was God" (John 1:1) and it still would be classified as expository if he devoted himself to explaining the actual meaning of the passage.

b. The extended passage.
John 1:1-14

A suggested outline is as follows: Statement of problem—What is the stress of the message that God wants to give to the world?

I. Who—tells of the person of Christ, (1-5, 14).

II. Why—indicates evidence which demands acceptance, (6-7).

III. How—demonstrates means of reception, 10-13.

2. SELECTED GROUP OF PASSAGES.

This method is employed when the speaker desires to examine what a number of Bible passages have to say on a subject. Those who use this approach tend to fall into three pitfalls. One is the failure to make a precise statement of the problem. Carelessness in this area can make the whole sermon incoherent. The second problem is the tendency to expound the same verses no matter what the subject. Many preachers have a number of "outstanding verses" committed to memory, and they just naturally come to mind when preparing sermons. The third temptation is an attempt to develop all the thoughts from a passage even though they may have nothing to do with the subject being treated.

Discipline is required to develop only the ideas which contribute to the solution of the stated problem and to leave some of the choice material for another sermon. Thus, the appropriate warnings for those using this approach are: 1.) Say exactly what you want to say in the statement of the problem; 2.) Be careful that the texts selected are the most applicable in solving the problem; 3.) From these Scriptures, choose only the ideas which contribute toward the stated goal.

The following sample outline makes use of a selected group of passages.

Statement of problem—Why did Jesus become man?

I. He became man in order to reveal the invisible God. "And the Word became flesh, and dwelt among us, and we beheld His glory, glory as of the only begotten from the Father, full of grace and truth" (John 1:14).

"No man has seen God at any time; the only begotten God, who is in the bosom of the Father, He has explained Him" (John 1:18).

II. He became man in order to obtain human experience.

A. In order to be an effective High Priest. "Therefore, He had to be made like His brethren in all things, that He might become a merciful and faithful high priest in things pertaining to God, to make propitiation for the sins of the people. For since He Himself was tempted in that which He has suffered, He is able to come to the aid of those who are tempted" (Hebrews 2:17, 18).

"Since then we have a great high priest who has passed through the heavens, Jesus the Son of God, let us hold fast our confession. For we do not have a high priest who cannot sympathize with our weaknesses, but one who has been tempted in all things as we are, yet without sin. Let us therefore draw near with confidence to the throne of grace, that we may receive mercy and may find grace to help in time of need" (Hebrews 4:14-16).

B. In order to be an effective judge. "And He gave Him authority to execute judgment, because He is the Son of Man" (John 5:27).

III. He became man in order to die as the God-man. "But we do see Him who has been made for a little while lower than the angels, namely, Jesus, because of the suffering of death crowned with glory and honor, that by the grace of God He might taste death for every one" (Hebrews 2:9).

IV. He became man in order to demonstrate the nature of life after death, that man can expect. "Because I live, you shall live also" (John 14: 19b).

NOTE: Only because Christ was resurrected in human form can we know the kind of life to which Christ was referring. Now look at a passage like Luke 24 which describes the body of Christ as he fellowshipped with the disciples following the resurrection.

PREPARATION OF THE OUTLINE

1. THE APPROACH.

The passage of Scripture has been chosen. How does the expositor approach that portion of the Word of God and secure from it the message God would have him proclaim? The first necessity is to understand what the passage says. If you search diligently you will discover a number of usable ideas. (Suggestions for obtaining these ideas can be found in Chapter III.) Record these ideas without regard to organization. If they are not written down there is a strong possibility they will be forgotten. (See appendix work sheet No. 1.) When you are satisfied that you have determined the proper meaning, the next step is to examine the ideas, searching for a unifying thrust. Ask yourself, "What purpose can be accomplished in the lives of the people which is in harmony with the intent of the selected portion of Scripture?"

The next step is to carefully state the problem, making sure that each word is the most meaningful, and that the idea is presented in a concise manner. It is best to state the problem in the form of a question or an incomplete sentence. This forces you to unify the main points of the sermon by having each point either answer the question or complete the sentence. It is impossible to separate the task of stating the problem from that of determining the points of the outline. The thoughts taken from the passage which become the main points of the outline must answer the question asked in the problem.

When considering a selected group of passages, the order of the development of the sermon may be modified by choosing the problem first. Then choose portions of Scripture which contribute to the solution of the problem. It is wise, however, to approach each passage with an honest desire to determine the true meaning of the passage. Never assume that a text says exactly what you always thought it said. After careful study you may find that some verses do not contribute to the purpose and others will need to be considered. Record the ideas as you study each portion. Following this procedure, re-examine the statement of the problem to determine if revision might be required. Then arrange the points, using the supporting Scriptures in the most efficient manner to answer the question at issue. (See appendix work sheet No. 2.)

2. THE TESTS OF AN OUTLINE.

An effective sermon outline should pass inspection on four critical tests: unity, progress, diversity, and balance. Ask yourself these questions:

—Is the outline unified, that is, does each point answer the question asked in the statement of the problem?

—Is the outline progressive, that is, does each main idea point toward a climax, building on the store of knowledge presented in the previous point?

—Is the outline diverse, that is, does each main point say something that is exclusively different from the others?

33

—Are the points balanced, that is, is there approximately equal importance and amount of time assigned to each?

3. COMMON PERILS.

The following suggestions will help you avoid some of the common perils in outlining.

1) Guard against the use of "and," or other conjunctions either in the statement of the problem or the points. This usually means you are having difficulty establishing unity.

2) State the points in a coordinate manner. When answering your problem be consistent in using either a word, phrase or a sentence for each main point, preferably with similar grammatical construction. This helps you meet the standard of unity and diversity. It also helps you remember the outline.

3) Discard a point if it doesn't contribute to the solution of the problem. Many preachers have difficulty discarding some "juicy morsel" that might be very appropriate in another context but will distract from the goal in the message at hand.

4) If you find that material could be placed under one point as well as another, the outline is failing the test of diversity. Revise the points so that each is different from the other.

4. THE DEVELOPMENT OF SUBPOINTS.

Many of the suggestions for the main points of the outline will also fit the subpoints including the tests for exactness.

Other recommendations are:

1) Each subpoint should be derived from the text. In the true exposition every idea comes directly from the passage. Support may come from other sources but not the basic thoughts.

2) Each subpoint should support the main point, which thus indirectly requires each subpoint to contribute to the solution of the problem.

3) The preacher preparing a thirty minute sermon should limit himself to the development of an overall total of five to seven ideas. Many sermons suffer from an attempt to present more ideas than there is time to develop.

4) Not every main point requires subpoints. Do not feel you have failed the test of balance if a main point is developed without subpoints. Comparatively equal weight can be achieved at times by extended development of a main point.

5. THE DEVELOPMENT OF THE IDEA.

The usual order of development of an idea is explanation, substantiation, illumination and transition.

1) First, explain the idea clearly, relating how the text presents the truth.

2) Add appropriate support in the form of Bible quotations, quotation of other authorities, statistics, or other sources.

3) Illuminate the point. Make the idea vivid and usable through anecdotes or personal experiences.

4) The transition suggests the wider implications of the idea. Point out how it relates to the other points in solving the stated problem.

The response of the listener following the development of an individual idea should be, "I understand it; I believe it; I am convinced it will be practical to me; and, I see its significance to the sermon as a whole."

6. WORDING OF THE OUTLINE.

It is a great help to the listener if *the words of the outline are derived directly from the text.* This helps him retain the thoughts and enables him to recall the sermon later, especially if he is encouraged to underline the words of the outline in his Bible. I John 3:23 reads: "And this is His commandment, that we believe in the name of His Son Jesus Christ, and love one another, just as He commanded us." An outline following the words of the text would be:

Statement of problem: How does God describe the balanced Christian life?

I. Believe in the name of His Son Jesus Christ.

II. Love one another.

Three sentences taken from Philippians 4:1-4 provide a further example:

Statement of problem: What are three commands which, if obeyed, would preserve unity among Christian workers?

I. Stand firm in the Lord (1).

II. Live in harmony in the Lord (2).

III. Rejoice in the Lord (4).

The prominence of the points is enhanced when you use the actual words of Scripture in your outline, even though they may require considerable explanation in the development of the sermon. Romans six is a common example. The words "know" or "knowing" occur in verses 3, 6, and 9. The command to "consider" is made in verse 11. The challenge to "present" is noted five times in verses 13, 16, 19. A suggested outline would be:

Statement of problem: What is God's prescription for overcoming sin?

I. To *know* (3, 6, 9).

II. To *consider* (11).

III. To *present* (13, 16, 19).

While it is of benefit to the listener to use the words of the Scriptures in outlining, you will find it necessary in most cases to *use your own words to express the idea of the text*. The goal of these statements is simplicity and clarity. Some speakers delight in finding words that begin with the same letter to form their outline. When this works with ease it may aid in gaining attention and even contribute to listener retention. However, if it is necessary to stretch the meaning of a word to make it fit, it can be damaging to the speaker's intent to present a precise thought. It is far better to sacrifice a rhythmic outline for saying exactly what you desire to communicate.

The following are examples of outlines where the preacher's own words express the ideas of the text.

1. Colossians 1:9-23.
   Statement of problem: What truths about Christ demand our allegiance?

   I. What Christ did (12-14).

   II. Who Christ is (15-19).

   III. What Christ plans to do (20-23).

2. II Corinthians 5:19, "Namely, that God was in Christ reconciling the world to Himself, not counting their trespasses against them, and He has committed to us the word of reconciliation."
   Statement of problem: What is the inspiration for a Christian to be missionary-minded?

   I. The example of incarnation: "God was in Christ."

   II. The message of reconciliation: "God was in Christ reconciling the world to Himself, not counting their trespasses against them."

   III. The commission to evangelization: "He has committed to us the word of reconciliation."

7. THE INTRODUCTION.

More sermons fail because the audience has not been prepared to receive the message than for any other single reason.

The three goals of an introduction are: 1) To secure favorable attention to the speaker; 2) To provide proper background information which will enable the audience to understand the message; 3) To awaken interest so that each member of the audience considers the message vital to himself.

Securing Favorable Attention

The faithful pastor who commands the respect of his congregation may have to do very little to secure the favorable attention of his audience. His own enthusiasm will help arouse the desired anticipation. The request that his audience turn to the Scripture to be considered may be sufficient to gain most of the people's attention. Some find it helpful to refer to some event involving the congregation, or some well known current event that relates to the subject to be discussed. Another possibility might be to commend the audience for some particular reason. An appropriate humorous incident can also be effective.

Some approaches produce unfavorable attention. Avoid *apologies*. This includes statements such as, "I haven't had much time to study," or "I know that my knowledge of this passage is extremely limited," or "I preached on this not long ago so I won't have much to say that's new to you." These can only produce an apathetic attitude toward what the speaker is about to say.

If you leave the introduction to the spur of the moment you will probably *ramble* in your opening words. Your statements will lack focus and give the impression that you are just taking up time. Relating a series of humorous references that have nothing to contribute to the purpose of the message can also produce an unfavorable response. Unless the audience has come to be entertained, they want the speaker to demonstrate that his purpose is to present a solid message which will be of lasting benefit.

Background Information

Presentation of proper background information for the understanding of the problem is essential. Always define unfamiliar terms, especially theological terms, but be careful not to overdo it. An acquaintance with the immediate and more extended context in which the text occurs is often essential to the exposition. Other types of background information that may prove helpful are the *historical background* of the text and the association of other *related passages of Scripture.*

Awakening Interest

The third goal of the introduction is to awaken the interest of the audience in the subject to be presented. When this step is achieved the audience is full of anticipation, because they know the speaker is going to answer a perplexing question. This is why the "statement of the problem" is so important. You must convince the audience of the urgency of solving the problem. This will force you to treat issues that are of vital concern. One lady was heard to complain, "Our pastor is always scratching where I don't itch."

The following common universal desires provide a basis for creating interest. These desires are:

1. to love others
2. to be loved by others
3. to be accepted by one's peers
4. to have peace of mind
5. to have health
6. to lead a meaningful life
7. to live without fear of death
8. to be protected from harm

9. to have job security
10. to accumulate knowledge
11. to have a happy family
12. to experience success in business

A few goals especially applicable to Christians are:
1. to find God's will for one's life
2. to learn, especially the Bible
3. to have a growing Christian experience
4. to deepen the fellowship with other Christians
5. to reach others for Christ
6. to guide one's family for the honor of Christ

There are many kinds of material you can use to create interest in the issue to be considered. Some of these are:

1. Quotations. Some recognized authority on the subject, a famous person, or a relatively unknown person who has made a significant statement stressing the importance of a subject can help awaken interest. Even a quotation from someone who has attacked or opposed a practice or doctrine can stress the need for consideration. For example, you might quote an astronaut telling of what prayer has meant to him. On the other hand, quoting someone who opposes the practice of prayer by the astronauts could become a challenge to Christians to take advantage of their privilege.

2. Current events. An event of common knowledge and concern can show the need for action by the believer. The news that a "church" dedicated to the worship of Satan has just been started in the community should be the basis for an appeal to renew our efforts to bear an impact on the area for Christ.

3. Questions. Emphasize the need for solving a problem by asking questions. Thought-provoking inquiry often demonstrates to the hearer his inadequate understanding. II Corinthians 5:16 reads, "Therefore from

now on we recognize no man according to the flesh; even though we have known Christ according to the flesh, yet now we know Him thus no longer." What does it mean "we recognize no man according to the flesh?"

When did they know "Christ according to the flesh?"

Does "we know him thus no longer" mean we will never see Christ again in the flesh?

You have aroused the listener's curiosity. He wants answers! Of course you must be able to answer the questions you raised!

4. Negatives. Point out an inadequate answer to a problem in order to stress the satisfactory solution.

Paul exhorted the Philippians to "work out your salvation with fear and trembling" (Philippians 2:12). Explain that this "salvation" is not salvation from sin. The word "salvation" means "deliverance." The type of deliverance must be interpreted according to the context. The problem from which the church in Philippi needed to be delivered was "selfishness" (2:3) and "grumbling" and "disputing" (2:14). If more churches were concerned about "deliverance" from these vices, the message of "deliverance" from sin would be much more attractive.

5. Reference to the time of year. The religious calendar including Lent, Easter, Pentecost Sunday, Thanksgiving, and Christmas provides occasion to stress the importance of the respective truths the different holidays are intended to memorialize. National holidays also can provide the springboard to stress a scriptural truth. The Fourth of July, for instance, can be compared to the declaration of independence available through Christ's work on our behalf.

6. Analogy. The imaginative speaker can find an abundance of events and illustrations to impress the audience with the importance of a truth. A war that continues without apparent willingness to attack the

41

enemy is analogous to the Christian who never has overcoming power in his Christian life. He refuses to deal decisively with the enemy of his soul even though he has been provided with the armor to do so.

The importance of giving careful attention to the introduction cannot be over emphasized. The time given to the presentation of it may vary greatly, however. Some subjects will be readily understood and considered vital by the audience. With others, an extensive job of salesmanship is a necessity. For a thirty minute message, spend from five to seven minutes on the introduction. The important consideration is not the time spent on it, but whether it accomplishes its purpose. Ask yourself three questions at the end of an introduction to see if it is effective.

1) Do I have a rapport with the audience so they want to hear what I have to say?

2) Do they have the background so they will understand what I have to say?

3) Are they convinced it is essential that they hear what I have to say?

Keep these three questions clearly in mind, but remember that in preparing the introduction there may be considerable overlapping. Relating the background material can arrest favorable attention. Arousing interest in a subject may at the same time produce attention and provide sufficient background material.

8. THE CONCLUSION.

Many speakers neglect to prepare the conclusion to the sermon, assuming that the inspiration of the moment at the climax of the sermon will provide a clue as to the best closing appeal. However, this rarely happens. Often, an otherwise effective sermon loses its impact because of a weak conclusion.

The conclusion usually is composed of two elements: a review of the message and the appeal to action. The purpose of the review is to recall the statement of the problem and the main points which have provided the answer to the problem. The appeal for a response on the part of the audience is made on the basis of that answer.

The question is sometimes asked as to how much application and appeal to action should be made throughout the message. If the audience has been sold on the fact that the statement of the problem is important to them, the need for constant application will be minimized. They will do it for themselves. Repeated applications in a message can have the same effect on an audience as overcorrecting a child. After awhile the listening ear is lost. It is usually better to build your case in the progress of the sermon and save the appeal to action until the conclusion. The amount of application in the body of the message will vary according to nature of the material and the goal of the message.

As you prepare the "statement of problem" keep in mind the action that you expect on the basis of the solution. The reasons stated for interest in the problem in the introduction can provide the basis for an appeal to action. For example if you are answering the question, "Why is Jesus God?" You might create interest by pointing out that one cannot meaningfully put Christ in the place of preeminence in his life unless he is certain that Jesus is God. The appeal in the conclusion would then be that since He is God, we should put Him in the place of preeminence in our lives, and then worship and serve Him.

Strive for a specific action. Often an audience is moved to do something but doesn't know how to go about it. If the appeal is to read the Bible, have a Bible reading plan available for distribution at the close of the meeting. If the appeal is for becoming a witness to others, announce a training class. Provide opportunity for the people to write their intentions for action on a decision card or receive counseling about how to implement their decision. Some ministers invite people to respond by coming forward, raising their hands for prayer, or requesting helpful literature. Whatever the method, direct people's attention to a specific response.

Some approaches to the conclusion are as follows:

1. Illustration—Use illustrations that unify the entire sermon and provide an appeal for action. For example, a dental assistant had witnessed to a dentist over a period of weeks. She was not sure he was grasping the idea until one day he asked her if she *really believed* that Jesus was God, that He died for the sins of all men, that all men are lost apart from Him, and that He is coming again to set up His kingdom. Her reply was a positive affirmation. His thought provoking analysis was, "Then you can't live like other people do, can you?" You can see the potential of this experience for audience motivation, especially if you have just emphasized the truths that were mentioned by the dentist.

2. Quotations — The statement of someone who has benefited from taking the action you are suggesting bears a great impact. This could be a comment from a Bible character who responded to the appeal. An observation from one who failed to take the action and suffered the consequences is another possibility. A quotation from a leader in another field who is taking similar action with much less motivation could be convicting. This might be a political leader, a social reformer, or almost any well-known personality.

3. Personal experiences—the personal testimony of the speaker that he has responded to the action he expects of the audience carries great weight. Also the account of others who have been observed responding to the suggested action can produce a positive response.

4. Reference to alternatives — A study of a number of messages of Billy Graham indicates that his most

common conclusion is to offer a choice. The listener is either going to be ready at the second coming or suffer the disastrous consequences. He can either choose Christ's way of life or the world's path to death. The listener is always forced to make a decisive choice.*

*   *   *

A few further suggestions in relation to the conclusion are:

1. Eliminate the statement, "in conclusion." This is the signal that the speaker has said all that is important and he is now going to make his final remarks. The announcement of the closing hymn is forthcoming.

2. Worse yet, never say "in conclusion" and then not conclude. Under the former suggestion interest is lost; with this practice brotherly love may be lost!

3. Rarely is it wise to introduce new exposition in the conclusion. This should be done in the body of the sermon.

4. Do not repreach the message in the conclusion. You may feel that the response is not quite what you expected but rehashing the ideas in the conclusion will not salvage it.

5. Refrain from apologies for apparent failure with such statements as, "I'm afraid I haven't made the point clear" or "I don't want to bore you with any more." Humility is an admirable trait but this is not the place to express it. It will only detract further from a positive impression.

6. The length of the conclusion for a thirty minute message should be approximately three to five minutes.

---

*Glenn O'Neal, "An Analytical Study of Certain Rhetorical Factors Used by Billy Graham in the 1949 Los Angeles Meetings." (Unpublished doctoral dissertation, The University of Southern California, Los Angeles, 1956), pp. 92-95.

This, of course, is subject to wide variation depending on the action expected and the type of material employed. There is no place, however, for the rambling conclusion that seemingly has no purpose and no end.

7. End on a positive note. The preacher can be an optimist because there is no place for gloom in the Christian message. Sin may be degrading but the power of Christ can transform. The situation in the world may be sad but better days are ahead. A note of triumph should be obvious in the conclusion.

9. TRANSITIONS

A transition in a sermon is that which relates one point to another. In preaching, the goal is to conclude each point with a statement that attaches the idea to the statement of the problem and then leads into the next main point. For example you might say, "We have pointed out that Jesus became man (the problem) in order to reveal the invisible God (point I). He also became man (the problem) in order to obtain human experience (point II)." Review in this manner before each main point and before the conclusion. These perspective transitions help the audience recognize the plan of sermon development and retain the ideas. They also prepare the audience for a favorable response to the action requested.

Some suggestions in regard to transitions are:

1. Do not assume the audience has followed the unfolding of the sermon. Attention lags and the mind wanders. The audience needs constant reminders of the progress that has already been made.

2. Vary the actual statement of the transition so the wording does not become mechanical. Some ministers merely state that "point one was" and "point two was," etc. Others preface each transition with "I have said. . . ." You can provide variety by carefully pre-

paring the transitions on the basis of the material presented.

3. State the transition concisely. Do not be guilty of reviewing the point in such detail that the perspective is lost.

4. Confine numbering to transitions between main points only. Confusion results when the subpoints are delineated by such statements as, "Now the third idea under point two is!" This does not mean that there are to be no transitions between subpoints. Their relation to the other ideas must be established, but not by numbering them.

5. Some pastors have found it helpful to list the main points and subpoints in the church bulletin as an aid to the audience in understanding the relationship of the ideas.

(For a sample form to aid in outlining, see appendix work sheet No. 2.)

CHAPTER III

GATHERING MATERIAL FOR THE FOR THE EXPOSITORY SERMON

GATHERING MATERIAL FOR THE EXPOSITORY SERMON

DETERMINING THE MEANING

The first task of the expositor is to determine the meaning. To do this he needs certain tools, such as, several versions of the Bible, a concordance, a Bible dictionary, commentaries including critical commentaries and lexicons for both the Hebrew Old Testament and Greek New Testament. A Hebrew Old Testament and a Greek New Testament with the ability to read them is helpful, but there are many able expositors whose knowledge of the original languages is limited. However, you should at least know enough about the languages to be able to use the resource material that is available.

Again, remember that recording the ideas as you discover them is essential if you want to retain them. The approach to gathering information may vary according to individual preference but the following are some of the ways to determine the meaning of a portion of Scripture.

1. Decide the proper word emphasis and inflection. Read and reread the passage to be certain you are interpreting it as the writer or speaker intended. This may require research into the background of the writer or the historical setting in which the passage was written. Scrutinize the context. Often the order of the words in the original language is indicative of word emphasis. It is estimated that in English there are at least fifty variations of the word "oh." It all depends on the inflection you use when you say it. That inflection is impossible to write and difficult to define. The Hebrews and the Greeks faced the same problem.

The verses below are listed with certain words underlined. Unless these words are emphasized with the proper inflections the meaning may be missed entirely.

Luke 24:25—"And He said to them, O foolish men and slow of heart to believe in *all* that the prophets have spoken!"

Luke 2:49—"And He said to them, Why is it that you were looking for Me? Did you not know that I had to be in *My* Father's house?"

Ephesians 3:8—"To me, the very least of all saints, this grace was given, to preach to the *Gentiles* the unfathomable riches of Christ."

Hebrews 2:3a—"How shall *we* escape if *we* neglect so great a salvation?"

Romans 6:1—"What shall *we* say then? Are *we* to continue in sin that grace might increase?"

I Corinthians 11:20—"Therefore when you meet together, it is not to eat the *Lord's* Supper."

I Timothy 2:8a—"Therefore I want the *men* in every place to pray. . . ."

2. Examine the passage from the standpoint of the exegesis of the original words.

a) Check the etymology of the word, especially key words in the exposition. Use helpful tools such as Kittel*, or Arndt and Gingrich† for the Greek, and Davidson‡ for the Hebrew.

b) Check the grammatical construction giving special attention to the verbs.

c) Check other translations of the word when it is employed in another context. To find such information consult an analytical concordance, or a work such as Vine's treatment of New Testament words.**

---

*G. Kittel, *Theological Dictionary of the New Testament,* 8 vols. when completed (Grand Rapids: Eerdmans, 1964).

†William F. Arndt and F. Wilbur Gingrich (ed.), *A Greek-English Lexicon of the New Testament and Other Early Christian Literature* (Chicago: The University of Chicago Press, 1957).

‡B. Davidson, *The Analytical Hebrew and Chaldee Lexicon* (London: Samuel Bagster and Sons Limited).

**W. E. Vine, *An Expository Dictionary of New Testament Words* (Westwood, New Jersey: Fleming H. Revell Company, 1940).

d) Check other versions to see how the word was translated in the same verse.

A few words of caution are in order for those who handle the original language. Do not give the impression that one cannot really understand the Bible unless he knows Hebrew and Greek. This is not true and statements or implications to this effect can discourage the listener. Show how the original deepens and clarifies the meaning, but it is unnecessary to declare, "Now if you knew the original language, you would understand that this means. . . ." It is far better to say, "This word could be translated. . . ," or "In another version the word was translated. . . ."

Do not be tempted to display your knowledge of the original languages. An interesting thought from the Greek or Hebrew is meaningless unless it contributes to the problem of the message. If you present information with the motivation of pride, you may engender the same fruit in the lives of your listeners. However, it is also important to avoid making dogmatic pronouncements on the basis of the meaning of an English word. One preacher was reported to have been preaching on faith and referred to Joseph as an example. The passage declares that Joseph "took unto him his wife; and knew her not till she had brought forth her firstborn son . . ." (Matthew 24:25a KJV). The application was reported to be, "Now there's an example of real faith. He married Mary before he even knew her!"

II Timothy 2:15 from the King James version reads, "Study to show thyself approved unto God, a workman that needeth not to be ashamed, rightly dividing the word of truth." To exhort your listeners to "study" from this passage is to miss the intent of the word. It literally means "make it one's aim" or "be diligent." The exhortation is intended to cause us to be concerned about the approval of God upon our lives.

Check the English dictionary for the variety of meanings of a word. This might give you a clue as to why the translator chose that particular word. Use of the tools to check the original languages is essential if you want to preach the truth of the Word with the assurance that you are communicating the intent of the writer.

3. Determine the correct punctuation. If you are qualified to do so, study the syntax of the original language. Consulting critical authorities and a variety of translations can provide clues to determining the correct punctuation.

Ephesians 1:7-10 is quoted below from the *King James Version* and the *New American Standard Bible* in order to emphasize the difference punctuation makes in determining the meaning.

"In whom we have redemption through his blood, the forgiveness of sins, according to the riches of his grace; wherein he hath abounded toward us in all wisdom and prudence; Having made known unto us the mystery of his will, according to his good pleasure which he hath purposed in himself: That in the dispensation of the fulness of times he might gather together in one all things in Christ, both which are in heaven, and which are on earth; even in him." (Ephesians 1:7-10 KJV)

"In Him we have redemption through His blood, the forgiveness of our trespasses, according to the riches of His grace, which He lavished upon us. In all wisdom and insight He made known to us the mystery of His will, according to His kind intention which He purposed in Him with a view to an administration suitable to the fulness of the times, that is, the summing up of all things in Christ, things in the heavens and things upon the earth. In Him . . ." (Eph. 1:7-10 NASB).

54

4. Analyze the passage carefully to see if you have overlooked any ideas. Often the expositor falls into the trap of accepting the usual interpretation which blinds his mind to a deeper meaning. An example of this might be I Timothy 1:12a where Paul expresses appreciation to the Lord for calling him to service, "even though I was formerly a blasphemer and a persecutor and a violent aggressor." The usual emphasis is that in spite of Paul's sordid past he was called to serve. But upon a closer examination of the word "blasphemer" one discovers an indirect proof for the deity of Christ. Paul, a devoted Pharisee, would never have spoken injuriously of God but he had done so to Christ. Thus what he is really saying is that there was a day when he spoke injuriously of God because he failed to give honor to Christ as God. Or consider Luke 22:54b which declares that "Peter was following at a distance." The fact that he was "at a distance" or "afar off" (KJV) is the ordinary emphasis. One must also remember that Peter was "following!"

5. Search for possible inferences from the passage. Many of the most usable *ideas* are those *inferred* from the passage. Several verses from II Timothy provide examples of inferences.

4:11b—"Pick up Mark and bring him with you, for he is useful to me for service." If this Mark is the same one Paul earlier refused to allow to accompany Barnabas and himself on a missionary journey, then it looks like Paul was willing to change his mind about a person who evidently had proven himself.

4:13—"When you come bring . . . the books, especially the parchments." The "books" and "parchments" were for study and writing respectively. The implication is that he kept busy; he was never satisfied with past attainments.

4:14—"Alexander, the coppersmith did me much harm; the Lord will repay him according to his deeds."

Paul apparently refused to allow bitterness and revenge over opposition to control his behavior. He left vengeance in the hands of the Lord.

4:16, 17a—"At my first defense no one supported me, but all deserted me; may it not be counted against them. But the Lord stood with me, and strengthened me. . . ." Paul had evidently learned to appreciate the presence of Christ to such an extent that it compensated for the disappointments caused by lack of support from fellow Christians.

4:18—"The Lord will . . . bring me safely to His heavenly kingdom; . . ." In spite of difficulties, Paul never lost the glow of the anticipation of having a share with Christ in the coming kingdom.

Almost every portion of Scripture lends itself to thought-provoking inference. Read what others have written about the text. This will provide many new ideas to help deepen the meaning of the Word and solve the problem of the individual message.

FOCUSING ATTENTION
ON THE MEANING

There are several ways a preacher can focus attention on the meaning and significance of a passage and maintain audience interest. Some of them are:

1. Read the passage incorrectly. For example, *substitute the wrong words.* This is most effective when the passage is well known and the error you insert is one commonly believed. Do not use this method so often that it becomes commonplace, but in the proper context it can be thought provoking and convicting.

Verses that lend themselves to word substitution might be:

Acts 5:40-42—"And they took his advice; and after calling the apostles in, they flogged them and ordered them to speak no more in the name of Jesus, and then released them. So they went on their way from the presence of the council, (substitution: complaining that they had been mistreated and declaring to the church that some other way of spreading the gospel would have to be found since witnessing was now illegal) rejoicing that they had been considered worthy to suffer shame for His name. And every day, in the temple and from house to house, they kept right on teaching and preaching Jesus as the Christ." By substituting a practice considered quite normal, the contrast of the spirit of the New Testament church is emphasized.

Titus 2:11, 12—"For the grace of God has appeared, bringing salvation to all men, instructing us (substitution: that we can do whatever we please and still be saved) to deny ungodiness and worldly desires and to live sensibly, righteously and godly in the present age." The idea that the grace of God encourages looseness of life is corrected by inserting what the passage does not say to make more vivid what it actually declares.

James 5:14—"Is anyone among you sick? Let him call for (substitution: the doctor) the elders of the church, and let them pray over him, anointing him with oil in the name of the Lord." The idea would not be to minimize the need for doctors, but to emphasize how little consideration is given to the scriptural exhortation to prayer for the sick.

Job 1:21b—"The Lord gave and the (substitution: devil) Lord has taken away. Blessed be the name of the Lord." Many people blame evil circumstances on the devil. Job counted what the Lord allowed, as coming from Him.

Another way to read a passage incorrectly is to *stop in the wrong place.* The Lord practiced this in the synagogue when he read from Isaiah 61:1, 2. (See Luke 4:16-21.) Check what Christ read with what is recorded in the Isaiah passage and you will discover that He stopped in the middle of the wording as the hearers were accustomed to having it expressed. Evidently he omitted "And the day of vengeance of our God" (Isaiah

61:2) because it was not his purpose to initiate that day at His first coming. He stopped in an unusual place to emphasize both the positive and negative goal of His coming.

Many people quote Matthew 11:28, "Come to Me, all who are weary and heavy laden, and I will give you rest." But they stop at the wrong place if they do not continue in the passage; not only heeding the admonition to "come," but to "take My yoke upon you and learn from Me" (29). In other words, there are those who desire the "rest" but not the "yoke."

What a gloomy prospect it would be for Israel if Luke 13:35 ended with the statement, "Behold, your house is left to you desolate." However, it is significant that the verse does not conclude there, but adds, "and I say to you, you shall not see Me until the time comes when you say, 'Blessed is He who comes in the name of the Lord!' " Thus, stopping before the thought is complete provides an opportunity to emphasize the truth recorded in the latter part of the passage.

2. Ask questions to help focus attention on the meaning. They can aid in expanding the breadth of an idea and establish inter-relationships with other ideas. For example:

John 21:15—"Simon, son of John, do you love Me more than these?" Why did Christ ask this question? No doubt He was referring to the rest of the disciples for Peter had declared in Mark 14:29, "Even though all may fall away, yet I will not." The Lord's reference to "these" was an attempt to gain the humble admission from Peter that his devotion was not greater than the other disciples.

I John 3:2—"Beloved, now we are children of God, and it has not appeared as yet what we shall be. We know that, if He should appear, we shall be like Him, (why?) because we shall see Him just as He is." The interpolation of "why?", especially preceding a "because," helps interpret properly the reasoning of the writer. In this case, it is interesting to conjecture that the reason Christians will be like Christ at His coming is that they will have an unhindered vision of Christ in all of His glory.

3. Paraphrase the passage. An expanded or a summary paraphrase often helps clarify the meaning. Illustrations of expanded paraphrase are:

John 14:8, 9—"Philip said to Him, 'Lord, show us the Father, and it is enough for us.' Jesus said to him, 'Have I been so long with you, and yet you have not come to know Me, Philip? He who has seen Me has seen the Father; how do you say, show us the Father?'" Expanded paraphrase: After Jesus had made ambitious claims about going to "prepare a place" for His disciples and providing the "way" for them to get there, Philip told the Lord that it would help to give assurance that he had the authority to make such claims if they could see God. Jesus was disappointed that Philip had not recognized from His teaching and miracles that He was God, and declared to Philip that the one who has seen *Him* has seen God. He wondered how Philip could still ask for further enlightenment.

Mark 10:18—"And Jesus said to Him, 'Why do you call Me good? No one is good except God alone.'" Expanded paraphrase: You call Me good. If I am a man, then you as a Jew, who knows that true goodness belongs only to God, cannot call Me good. Thus a passage that might appear on the surface to give justification for wondering if Christ was disclaiming deity, is clarified by paraphrase to show that it actually teaches the opposite.

A summary paraphrase can be used when you want to simplify an extended passage by stating the whole idea in a few words.

Philippians 2:5-11—"Have this attitude in yourselves which was also in Christ Jesus, who, although He existed in the form of God, did not regard equality with God a thing to be grasped, but emptied Himself, taking

59

the form of a bond-servant, and being made in the likeness of men. And being found in appearance as a man, He humbled Himself by becoming obedient to the point of death, even death on a cross. Therefore also God highly exalted Him, and bestowed on Him the name which is above every name, that at the name of Jesus every knee should bow, of those who are in heaven, and on earth, and under the earth, and that every tongue should confess that Jesus Christ is Lord, to the glory of God the Father." Summary paraphrase: This can be summarized in three steps—Christ stooped from heaven to humanity, from humanity to death, and then was exalted from death to glory.

4. Introduce a supposition, suggesting what would be the case if the opposite were true. Paul used this method in I Corinthians 15:12-19 where he suggests the alternatives to belief in the resurrection of Christ. Another example is the supposition that Christ was not born of a virgin, which leaves us with the option of Joseph being his father, or illegitimacy. Joseph said Jesus was not his child (Matthew 1:19-25). Thus the only alternative to the virgin birth is that his father is unknown. Use this stratagem to focus attention on the importance of the truth presented.

5. Deal with wrong interpretations. Recognizing how others have misinterpreted a Scripture can help the Bible student to emphasize the truth of a passage. Some verses that can be treated in this manner are:

Colossians 1:15—"And He is the image of the invisible God, the first-born of all creation." Explanation: Some people interpret "the image of the invisible God" as an indication that Christ was only the "image" not "God." But when understood as the "visible image" of the "invisible God," the idea of God in human form becomes obvious and thus His deity is established. The second phrase in the passage, "the first-born of all creation," is sometimes used to establish the fact that Christ was the first to be created. "First-born," however, when properly understood, indicates authority or position and has nothing to do with origin. In fact, verse seventeen declares, "He is before all things."

Romans 14:7—"For not one of us lives for himself, and not one dies for himself." Explanation: To many people this verse forms the basis for an appeal to live a life of consideration for our fellow-man. The intent of the passage, however, is to emphasize our obligation to God. The next statement reads, "for if we live, we live for the Lord."

Colossians 2:21—"Do not handle, do not taste, do not touch!" Explanation: These commands have been adopted by some as a motto to warn against the evils of alcohol. While most people recognize the curse that liquor has brought on our society, yet this passage should not be the basis for condemnation. If properly interpreted it says that we should no longer "submit . . . to decrees, such as, do not handle, etc." Thus, to use this verse as an argument against the use of alcohol violates both the meaning and the context.

II Corinthians 5:16—"Therefore from now on we recognize no man according to the flesh; even though we have known Christ according to the flesh, yet now we know Him thus no longer." Explanation: At least one system of theology bases its rejection of the believers' future resurrection in physical bodies and the appearance of Christ in physical form on these statements. Evidently, however, Paul was referring to a problem mentioned in I Corinthians 1:12 which indicates that the church was divided over loyalty to leaders, namely, Paul, Apollos, Cephas and Christ. Some in the church evidently knew Christ in the flesh and were not afraid to make the fact known! A paraphrase of the passage and verse seventeen might be: A man is not to be recognized as important on the basis of what past leader he is following. Even if one knew Christ in the flesh, He is now

61

gone. The important matter is your present relationship to Christ as a new creation. The old relationships no longer count. The new day to day relationship to Christ should be vital.

6. Determine the background of the passage. It is essential to research the background of the passage in order to prepare the introduction. In addition, this research often produces ideas that can be used to solve the problem. Historical considerations, the context and other Bible passages help illuminate the portion being studied.

a) Discover the historical background. A study of the history of Israel and the nation with which Israel was involved is extremely helpful to the expositor. Much resource material is available in Bible encyclopedias, and geographies.

Verses that emphasize the benefits of diligent research are:

Isaiah 6:1—"In the year of King Uzziah's death I saw the Lord sitting on a throne, lofty and exalted, with the train of his robe filling the temple." Historical background: Uzziah was a good king even though he died under discouraging circumstances. Assyria was threatening Israel and Uzziah's sons lacked the qualifications necessary to lead the people. Prospects for the future of Israel were bleak indeed. Thus, there may be added significance to the statement, "In the year of King Uzziah's death, I saw the Lord." Perhaps God was using a disturbing political situation to cause Isaiah to look to Him for a new vision of His glory and power.

Philippians 4:22—"All the saints greet you, especially those of Caesar's household." Historical background: Paul was in prison and the wicked Nero was in power. Paul was witnessing among the servants in what appeared to be the most unlikely place to find a reception for the gospel. But the saints among the servants of Nero sent greetings.

Romans 13:1—"Let every person be in subjection to the governing authorities. For there is no authority except from God, and those which exist are established by God." Historical background: The fact that Nero, a persecutor of Christians, was in power adds emphasis to the responsibility of Christians to give allegiance to the government.

Ephesians 4:1a—"I therefore, the prisoner of the Lord." Historical background: Paul was in prison in Rome. However, he calls himself "the prisoner of the Lord." Evidently his attitude was that even though Rome put him there, if the Lord allowed it, then he was His prisoner, not Rome's.

b) Search the context. Before selecting an individual text read carefully the related portion of Scripture which sometimes involves the entire book. Interpret each verse in light of the verses surrounding it.

The tenth chapter of John is an example of a passage which is impossible to interpret without careful attention to the context. A paraphrase of John 10:1-11 follows:

"There are thieves and robbers who are attempting to destroy my fold, Israel, like those who put the blind man out of the synagogue for admitting that I had healed his eyes. They who enter the fold in this manner are not coming as God intended. I am the true Shepherd of Israel; the one who is presenting the proper credentials according to Old Testament prophecies to enter into the fold of Israel. The true watchers of the flock of Israel, like John the Baptist and others, recognize my credentials and let me call the true seekers of God out of the fold of Israel. These true seekers, like the blind man who was healed, have ears attuned to my voice. They didn't understand Christ's words so he tried to clarify the message. He declared that he was the door by which the true sheep should come out of the fold of Israel and enter into the door of salvation. Inside that door they would enjoy the constant provision of Christ. The wicked priests are only interested in themselves and are destroying those in the fold. I am come to lay down my life in order that the people might enjoy an abundant life."

Understanding of the context involving the blind man, the selfish priests and the fold of Israel are essential considerations in the interpretation of this passage.

Ecclesiastes is a book that requires contextual considerations. The book was written by Solomon and presents the thinking of a man "under the sun" (1:3). He tries various avenues to find peace and purpose but each effort ends in despair. If individual statements of the distraught author are quoted as though they were spoken by God, without reference to the overall purpose of the book, all sorts of fanciful doctrines can be established. For example in 9:5 the statement is made, "For the living know they will die, but the dead do not know anything, nor have they any longer a reward; for their memory is forgotten."

Not only must the historical and contextual backgrounds be considered, but attention must be given to the inter-relationship with other passages of Scripture. A topical Bible helps you find a number of passages on the same subject as the one you are studying. Three categories of Scriptures may contribute to your grasp of a passage: *explanatory, supplementary* and *confirmatory.*

The *explanatory text* helps clarify an idea which otherwise might be difficult to understand. John 3:5 declares that ". . . unless one is born of water and the Spirit, he cannot enter into the kingdom of God." Various explanations are given for what is meant by "water." When Nicodemus requested an explanation of the teaching, Jesus answered, "Are you the teacher of Israel, and do not understand these things?" This indicates that there was an Old Testament reference which would help Nicodemus understand Christ's words. Ezekiel 36:25-27 explains what Christ must have had in mind. "Then I will sprinkle clean water on you, and you will be clean; I will cleanse you from all your filthiness and from all your idols. Moreover, I will give you a new heart and put a new spirit within you; and I will remove the heart of stone from your flesh and give you a heart of flesh. And I will put My Spirit within you and cause you to walk in My statutes, and you will be careful to observe My ordinances." The indication from Ezekiel is that the "water" denotes cleansing. This is the simplest interpretation and is corroborated by Titus 3:5 which reads, "He saved us, not on the basis of deeds which we have done in righteousness, but according to His mercy, by the *washing of regeneration* and renewing by the Holy Spirit."

Another example of one verse helping to explain another is the light thrown on Revelation 5:1ff by Jeremiah 32:9-14. Revelation 5:1 states, "And I saw in the right hand of Him who sat on the throne a book written inside and on the back, sealed up with seven seals." This verse is strategic to the understanding of the book of Revelation. The search begins for the person "worthy" to open the "book" and the next several chapters record the extended procedure of opening the seals.

The Jeremiah passage presents the account of the purchase of a field by Jeremiah and explains the procedure in drawing up a title deed. "And I signed and sealed the deed, and called in witnesses, and weighed out the silver on the scales. Then I took the deeds of purchase, both the sealed copy containing the terms and conditions, and the open copy" (Jeremiah 32:10-11). Evidently part of the title deed was "open," describing the person who was qualified to open the seals and claim possession of the property. This explains the search in

Revelation for the one who was qualified to claim the kingdom (see Revelation 11:15) and the joy at discovering that "the Lion that is from the tribe of Judah, the Root of David, has overcome so as to open the book and its seven seals" (Revelation 5:5).

The epistles of Peter and John are filled with references to experiences with Christ which illuminate the passages written at the later date. This is especially true of Peter. The experience on the mount of transfiguration recorded in Matthew 17:1-8 helps clarify II Peter 1:16-18 which states, "For we did not follow cleverly devised tales when we made known to you the power and coming of our Lord Jesus Christ, but we were eyewitnesses of His majesty. For when He received honor and glory from God the Father, such an utterance as this was made to Him by the Majestic Glory, 'This is My beloved Son with whom I am well-pleased,'— and we ourselves heard this utterance made from heaven when we were with Him on the holy mountain." Events in the life of Paul recorded in the book of Acts help us interpret his epistles. There are many such references.

A *supplementary text* supplies details which are omitted from other texts especially the gospels. For instance if you read only Mark 15:32 you would conclude that both of the two men crucified with Christ rejected Him with no repentance. Mark says simply that ". . . those who were crucified with Him were casting the same insult at Him." However, Luke 23:39-43 reads, "And one of the criminals who were hanged there was hurling abuse at Him, saying, 'Are You not the Christ? Save Yourself and us!' But the other answered, and rebuking him said, 'Do you not even fear God, since you are under the same sentence of condemnation? And we indeed justly, for we are receiving what we deserve for our deeds; but this man has done nothing wrong.' And he was saying, 'Jesus, remember me when You come in Your kingdom.' And He said to him, 'Truly I say to you, today you shall be with Me in Paradise.'"

Confirmatory texts are used when you need the weight of several Scripture references to substantiate a truth. A series of verses that establish the "Word" as an agent of cleansing are as follows:

Ephesians 5:26—"That He might sanctify her, having cleansed her by the washing of water with the word."

John 15:3—"You are already clean because of the word which I have spoken to you."

Psalm 119:9—"How can a young man keep his way pure? By keeping it according to Thy Word."

＊　　＊　　＊

To use other texts most effectively:

a) Choose only the texts that clearly support the point. If you have to clarify a passage that is intended to clarify, your purpose has been defeated.

b) Refrain from developing other good ideas in a supporting text. Confine your emphasis to that which relates to your point.

c) Be careful not to over-support an idea.

d) Plan to have the audience turn to only a few supporting verses, usually a maximum of four, apart from the sermon text itself. If you ask your audience to turn to too many passages they may become frustrated and drop their attention.

e) Quote some verses so the audience does not have to turn to every Scripture.

f) Carefully mark the portions to be read so you can find them immediately.

g) Resist the temptation to use an abundance of supporting passages as a substitute for an in-depth study of the passage you are expounding.

ILLUSTRATING THE SERMON

The ability of any speaker to communicate truth is determined to a great extent by his creative and diligent use of illustrations to make ideas vivid. Christ's effective use of illustrations should challenge every minister to look for appropriate illustrations wherever they may be found.

Some of the sources of illustrations are:

1. The Bible—After relating an Old Testament experience Paul declares, "Now these things happened to them as an example, and they were written for our instruction, upon whom the ends of the ages have come" (I Corinthians 10:11). Constant study of the entire Bible reveals an abundant supply of illustrations on every subject. They help teach the living Word by making ideas come to life.

Christ often referred to Old Testament events in order to impress the hearers with a truth.

Luke 4:25-27—"But I say to you in truth, there were many widows in Israel in the days of Elijah, when the sky was shut up for three years and six months, when a great famine came over all the land; and yet Elijah was sent to none of them, but only to Zarephath, in the land of Sidon, to a woman who was a widow. And there were many lepers in Israel in the time of Elisha the prophet; and none of them was cleansed, but only Naaman the Syrian." These illustrations were evidently effective in establishing the point, for the next verses read, "And all in the synagogue were filled with rage as they heard these things; and they rose up and cast Him out of the city, . . ." (4:28-29a).

Luke 17:26-30—"And just as it happened in the days of Noah, so it shall be also in the days of the Son of Man: they were eating, they were drinking, they were marrying, they were being given in marriage, until the day that Noah entered the ark, and the flood came and

68

destroyed them all. It was the same as happened in the days of Lot: they were eating, they were drinking, they were buying, they were selling, the were planting, they were building; but on the day that Lot went out from Sodom it rained fire and brimstone from heaven and destroyed them all. It will be just the same on the day that the Son of Man is revealed."

2. Personal Experiences—There is a false notion in some Christian circles that a preacher should not relate personal experiences in the pulpit. Hence, one often hears the statement, "If you'll pardon the personal illustration." An apology like that is unnecessary. If an experience needs an apology, do not tell it; if it doesn't need an apology, a statement like that will weaken its effectiveness.

Avoid telling experiences that exalt yourself or your family. If you relate mistakes as well as victories, this danger is largely eliminated.

For a number of reasons personal experiences are the best source of illustrations. They have the advantage of being *new*. Those who hear a variety of preachers over an extended period of time sometimes feel like the ministers must be using the same sources for their illustrations. The same story crops up time after time. Some stories would be better filed in the archives. When you tell your own experiences, this problem is remedied.

Personal experiences are *interesting*. When attention lags, reference to some personal experience usually awakens an immediate response.

Personal experiences are *easy to relate*. Since you know the details of the event, you can talk about it with confidence. To most people, standing before an audience is a frightening experience at best. Telling a story you know well helps both you and your audience relax. However, be sure to review details of the event before you talk about it. Do not depend on the spur of the moment for recall. Carefully prepare presentation of a personal experience to avoid uncertainty and unnecessary details.

Christ and the *Bible writers* used personal experiences to present truth. As previously stated, the priests who excommunicated the blind man in John nine formed the basis for a message about false shepherds in chapter ten of John. Christ said to the multitude, ". . . you seek Me, not because you saw signs, but because you ate of the loaves, and were filled" (John 6:26). After reminding them of the feeding of the 5,000, he then established a point by commanding, "Do not work for the food which perishes, but for the food which endures to eternal life, which the Son of Man shall give to you . . ." (John 6:27). Peter related the vision of Acts ten, and presented a challenge on the basis of it in chapter eleven. Paul gave a personal testimony of his conversion experience on several occasions (see Acts 9, 22, and 26).

Where can you find personal illustrations? Each person has a store of personal experiences peculiar to him. Constantly *review your past life* looking for experiences which might be applicable to scriptural truth. The following suggestions are not intended to be exhaustive, but hopefully will awaken your imagination to potential sources of personal experiences. Some possibilities are:

a) Childhood relationships.

Such relationships include events that were especially impressive, occasions when you learned important lessons, your parents' efforts to teach through love and discipline, competition between brothers and sisters, and occurrences involving teachers and fellow students at school.

b) Events peculiar to native area.

Whether you grew up on the farm or in the city, you no doubt had many experiences which make good illustrations. The farmer is involved with animals, water (whether by rain or irrigation), fertilizing, sowing, weeding, spraying and harvesting. The city dweller knows about playground activities, hobbies, odd jobs, gardening, lawn care, problems caused by living in close proximity to others and, possibly, changing neighborhoods.

Become acquainted with problems peculiar to the area in which you are ministering. Get involved, at least in a minor way, with the activities common to your listeners. Learn their terminology. To be a novice is excusable. Sometimes it is even an advantage if your audience feels that its knowledge is superior to yours in some areas of experience. But, to remain in ignorance of the interests of the people to whom one is ministering, that is unpardonable.

c) Athletics.

The Apostle Paul constantly used athletic competition as a source of personal illustrations. His references were mostly to runners. In the United States you can add football, basketball, baseball, golf, fishing, hunting and other activities as sources of illustrations. The only requirement is that the average audience must know enough about the sport to make reference to it effective.

d) The pastoral ministry.

Pastoral activities are a ready source of meaningful experiences. Among these are church administrative and social responsibilities, pastoral counseling, weddings, funerals, personal witnessing and relationships with other ministers. However, avoid revealing conversations which would embarrass your listeners or make them feel you cannot keep confidences.

e) Travel.

Travel at home and in foreign countries often produces interesting situations. How did you travel? By car? Train? Airplane? Camel? Dogsled? What situations did you encounter that were peculiar to life in that country? Such subjects as native customs, the language barrier, treatment of foreigners and laws relating to tourists often make interesting illustrations for a sermon.

f) The home and family.

The events involved in running a home and raising a family is common knowledge, but its very commonness makes it potential illustration materal. Buying, selling and maintaining a house, produces problems common to nearly everyone. Mention your relationship to your children and you usually gain a ready response from the parents in the audience. Reference to any of the modern conveniences, from the telephone to the electric tooth brush, awakens a respondent chord.

g) Experiences that are created.

It is possible to create your own experiences. Ask your barber or your butcher what he thinks about a moral question or a scriptural truth. His answer could provide valuable illustration material.

h) Personal experiences of others.

Take advantage of the experiences of others as a source of personal illustrations. Preface the story with a statement such as, "A friend of mine related to me the following experience—." Never tell the story as if it happened to you. Be sure to tell it as it actually happened. If it is appropriate to the point you are trying to emphasize, it will be effective even though it did not happen to you.

3. Nature—Christ frequently used the phenomena of nature to make vivid the truths He presented. Here are a few of them which Matthew records:

6:22-23—"The lamp of the body is the eye; if therefore your eye is clear, your whole body will be full of light. But if your eye is bad, your whole body will be full of darkness. If therefore the light that is in you is darkness, how great is the darkness!"

6:26-30—"Look at the birds of the air, that they do not sow, neither do they reap, nor gather into barns; and yet your heavenly Father feeds them. Are you not worth much more than they? And which of you by

72

being anxious can add a single cubit to his life's span? And why are you anxious about clothing? Observe how the lilies of the field grow; they do not toil nor do they spin, yet I say to you that even Solomon in all his glory did not clothe himself like one of these. But if God so arrays the grass of the field, which is alive today and tomorrow is thrown into the furnace, will He not much more do so for you, O men of little faith?"

8:20—"The foxes have holes, and the birds of the air have nests; but the Son of Man has nowhere to lay His head."

13:3—"And He spoke many things to them in parables, saying, 'Behold, the sower went out to sow. . . .'"

13:24-25—"He presented another parable to them, saying, 'The kingdom of heaven may be compared to a man who sowed good seed in his field. But while men were sleeping, his enemy came and sowed tares also among the wheat, and went away."

13:31—"He presented another parable to them, saying, 'The kingdom of heaven is like a mustard seed, which a man took and sowed in his field. . . .'"

13:47—"Again, the kingdom of heaven is like a dragnet cast into the sea, and gathering fish of every kind. . . ."

16:1-3—"And the Pharisees and Sadducees came up, and testing Him asked Him to show them a sign from heaven. But He answered and said to them, 'When it is evening, you say, "It will be fair weather, for the sky is red." And in the morning, "There will be a storm today, for the sky is red and threatening." Do you know how to discern the appearance of the sky, but cannot discern the signs of the times?'"

24:32-33—"Now learn the parable from the fig tree: when its branch has already become tender, and puts forth its leaves, you know that summer is near; even so you too, when you see all these things, recognize that He is near, right at the door."

The characteristics of snow, the growth of plant life, the beauty of the mountains, rivers and the sea, as well as the intricacies of the human body, make beautiful pictures with potential for illustrating spiritual truths.

4. Current Events—Every preacher should be aware of the news of the day and constantly ask himself how he can use a current event or news item to focus on an idea from the Word.

Christ referred to two current experiences to establish a point in Luke 13:1-5. "Now on the same occasion there were some present who reported to Him about the Galileans, whose blood Pilate had mingled with their sacrifices. And He answered and said to them, 'Do you suppose that these Galileans were greater sinners than all other Galileans, because they suffered this fate? I tell you, no, but unless you repent, you will all likewise perish. Or do you suppose that those eighteen on whom the tower in Siloam fell and killed them, were worse culprits than all the men who live in Jerusalem? I tell you, no, but, unless you repent, you will all likewise perish.' "

The best time to use a news item is the week it happens so it is fresh in the minds of your listeners. This means that newspapers, news magazines and newscasts are ready sources for such material. Keep your mind fertile. As you read or listen to the news, constantly ask yourself, "How can I take advantage of this item in my preaching?" The need to stay up-to-date makes it difficult to file such material for future use. However, some items lend themselves to use at any time, for example, court battles, elections, legislative issues, riots, wars, activities of famous people, and items that bear directly on doctrinal or moral issues. File these for future reference.

5. Parables—A parable is an imaginary event that could take place and is commonly known to have taken place. Christ used this type of illustration often. He

spoke of "the sower" who "went out to sow" (Matthew 13:3), "a judge who did not fear God, and did not respect man" (Luke 18:2), and of "a certain nobleman" who "went to a distant country to receive a kingdom for himself, and then return" (Luke 19:12). It is obvious that He created each of these stories from experiences which all recognized as possible, in order to give more impact to His message. By using this method you can make up your own illustrations. For example, you can preface a story in such a manner that it is obvious you are making it up. Say, "Suppose a man owes a debt of $5,000.00, and another man puts $5,000.00 to his account." Or, merely say, "A man gets up in the morning, eats breakfast, gets in his car, etc." This method of illustration has unlimited possibilities.

6. Fables—A number of fables have been passed on from one generation to another. Because many of them are generally known, they can be quite effective if the story you choose lends itself to the emphasis of spiritual truth.

Two examples of these are:

A woodpecker was pecking away all day on a tree, not making much headway, but working hard at it. Along toward evening a thunderstorm came up. A bolt of lightning struck the tree, splitting it from top to the bottom, knocking the woodpecker to the ground. As he recovered from the stunning blow, he shook his head, looked at the tree and exclaimed, "Boy, that was some peck!" You can apply this fable to the person who is prone to take credit for work only God can do.

A second example is that of the dogs who were arguing over which could run the fastest. When a rabbit hopped by, the most outspoken boaster was challenged by the other dogs to prove his superiority and catch the rabbit. He gave chase, but soon returned shamefaced in failure. "You must remember that the rabbit was running for his life," the dog reasoned. "I was only running for my supper." Application: the extent of our motivation determines the zeal with which we serve Christ.

7. Persons—Christ used a child to teach an important lesson about humility.

Matthew 18:1-4—"At that time the disciples came to Jesus, saying, 'Who then is greatest in the kingdom of heaven?' And He called a child to Himself and stood him in their midst, and said, 'Truly I say unto you, unless you are converted and become like children, you shall not enter the kingdom of heaven. Whoever then humbles himself as this child, he is the greatest in the kingdom of heaven.' "

8. Objects—One of the most vivid examples of the use of objects to present a truth is in the communion service where Christ takes the bread and the cup to symbolize His body and His blood.

Matthew 26:26-28—"And while they were eating, Jesus took some bread, and after a blessing, He broke it and gave it to the disciples, and said, 'Take, eat; this is My body.' And He took a cup and gave thanks, and gave it to them, saying, 'Drink from it, all of you; for this is My blood of the covenant, which is to be shed on behalf of many for forgiveness of sins.' "

9. Charts and Pictures—Teaching through the eye gate is a valuable way to present truth. The overhead projector, film, film strip, and video tape make visual aids easy to use. Use them often!

10. Brief Comparisons—Develop the art of using brief comparisons or "windows." Some think of illustrations only in terms of extended stories, but attention to constant shorter comparisons is essential to maintain interest and make ideas come to life.

Some Scripural examples of these are:

Psalm 42:1—"As the deer pants for the water brooks, So my soul pants for Thee, O God."

Isaiah 40:31a—"Yet those who wait for the Lord will gain new strength; They will mount up with wings like eagles. . . ."

Psalm 72:6—"May he come down like rain upon the mown grass, Like showers that water the earth."

Matthew 17:20b—"If you have faith as a mustard seed, you shall say to this mountain, 'Move from here to there,' and it shall move; and nothing shall be impossible to you."

The hymn writers frequently use comparisons such as the simile, "Like a river glorious is God's perfect peace, . . ." and the hyperbole, "On Christ, the solid Rock, I stand; all other ground is sinking sand. . . ."

Compare a person whose confidence is dependent on keeping the law for salvation to the feeling one has when a police car, with red light flashing, approaches from the rear. One is never sure he has kept all the law.

Point out the similarities between the person who decides he will gradually break with sin in his life, to the boy who wanted to cut his dog's tail off, but thought it would hurt too much to cut it off all at once, so he decided to do it an inch at a time!

11. Science—The field of science is vast and fruitful in providing illustrations, but be sure the statements you make are accurate. If you are well acquainted with any area of science avoid becoming too technical in your illustrations. Remember that the communication of Scripture is your ultimate goal. Use words people can understand.

12. History and Archaeology—Every age of history is filled with incidents that lend themselves to vividly portraying truth. Especially is this true of the time of Christ and the Reformation period. Probably more people are acquainted with the events in those two ages than any other time in history. Archaeological discov-

eries which throw light on the background of Scripture are especially interesting.

* * *

In conclusion, here are some general suggestions about illustrations to remember:

Watch for illustrations. When you observe a possibility, record it.

Start an illustration file. When you check the file later, some may not be usable, but they may start you thinking about another experience that fits the occasion.

Master the illustration so that its progress and point are clear. Be concise, but be sure you make clear how it relates to the main idea.

Don't introduce a story by announcing you are going to illustrate a point. Plunge right into it. If it fits, it will be recognized; if not, telling them it is an illustration won't help!

Be certain that the vividness of the illustration doesn't raise other problems and sidetrack audience on issues other than the point you want to drive home.

Never say anything that could be considered morally in bad taste.

Check your sermon after you have prepared it to make sure there is no period longer than two minutes without at least a brief "window."

Illustrations that reflect unfavorably upon a particular racial or social group are in bad taste. Avoid them.

(For a sample form for recording ideas, see appendix work sheet No. 1.)

CHAPTER IV

TYPES OF OUTLINES

TYPES OF OUTLINES

Those who advocate the problem-solution approach to sermon preparation are sometimes accused of producing stereotyped, monotonous sermons. This does not need to be true. Wide variation in sermons is possible without violating either the method or the Scriptures.

This chapter contains several types of outlines which use the problem-solution approach, yet can hardly be considered stereotyped or monotonous. Analyze the outlines and you will notice that the types of outlines are not always mutually exclusive. Some outlines might fit under two different categories which further demonstrates the versatility of the problem-solution approach.

The types of problem-solution outlines we will consider in this chapter include outlines—

derived from an accumulation of evidence

that demonstrate reasoning from cause to effect

that employ an analogy

that present a pattern

that emphasize a contrast

that teach from an example

that give an explanation

that stress instruction

whose main points are component parts of a whole

which establish conditions

that challenge one to accept responsibility

whose main points embody interrogation

whose main points move in a time sequence

that describe something.

OUTLINES DERIVED FROM AN ACCUMULATION OF EVIDENCE

The accumulation of evidence is a form of inductive reasoning in which you establish a general premise by presenting ideas that substantiate it.

Example 1.

Scripture: Mark 10:45—"For even the Son of Man did not come to be served, but to serve, and to give His life a ransom for many."

Statement of Problem: How does Jesus demonstrate that it is not beneath His kingly dignity to become a servant?

I. By becoming man—"For even the Son of Man. . ."

II. By serving—". . . did not come to be served, but to serve. . . ."

III. By giving His life—". . . and to give His life a ransom for many."

Example 2.

Scripture: II Timothy 1:9-14

Statement of Problem: What is the basis for the assurance that one possesses eternal life?

I. Based on a logical explanation of historical facts. II Timothy 1:9-10—"Who has saved us, and called us with a holy calling, not according to our works, but according to His own purpose and grace which was granted us in Christ Jesus from all eternity, but now has been revealed by the *appearing* of our Savior Christ Jesus, who *abolished death,* and brought *life and immortality to light through the gospel."*

II. Based on a personal acquaintance with Christ. II Timothy 1:12—"For this reason I also suffer these things, but I am not ashamed; for *I know* whom I have believed and I am convinced that He is able to guard what I have entrusted to Him until that day."

III. Based on the indwelling power of the Holy Spirit. II Timothy 1:14—"Guard through the Holy Spirit who dwells in us, the treasure which has been entrusted to you."

Example 3.

Scripture: Luke 23:27-35
Statement of Problem: How was the love of Christ evidenced at the cross?

I. He urged the women to weep for themselves instead of Him.
Luke 23:27-28—"And there were following Him a great multitude of the people, and of women who were mourning and lamenting Him. But Jesus turning to them said, 'Daughters of Jerusalem, stop weeping for Me, but weep for yourselves and for your children.' "

II. He prayed for the salvation of those who placed Him on the cross.
Luke 23:34—"But Jesus was saying, 'Father forgive them; for they do not know what they are doing.' "

III. He refused to save Himself in the light of what He was accomplishing for others.
Luke 23:35—"And the people stood by, looking on. And even the rulers were sneering at Him, saying, 'He saved others; let Him save Himself if this is the Christ of God, His Chosen One.' "

Example 4.

Scripture: Galatians 2, 3.
Statement of Problem: How do we know salvation is free?

I. The purpose of the law demands that it be free.
Galatians 2:21—"I do not nullify the grace of God;

for if righteousness comes through the Law, then Christ died needlessly."
Galatians 3:21-22—"Is the Law then contrary to the promises of God? May it never be! For if a law had been given which was able to impart life, then righteousness would indeed have been based on law. But the Scripture has shut up all men under sin, that the promise by faith in Jesus Christ might be given to those who believe."

II. The work on the cross demands that it be free.
Galatians 2:21—"I do not nullify the grace of God; for if righteousness comes through the Law, then Christ died needlessly."
Galatians 3:13—"Christ redeemed us from the curse of the law, having become a curse for us—for it is written, 'Cursed is everyone who hangs on a tree.' "

III. The language of Scripture demands that it be free.
Galatians 2:16—"Nevertheless knowing that a man is not *justified* by the works of the Law but through faith in Christ Jesus, even we have believed in Christ Jesus, that we may be *justified* by faith in Christ, and not by the works of the Law; since by the works of the Law shall no flesh be justified."
Galatians 3:6—"Even so Abraham believed God, and it was *reckoned to him as righteousness.*"

IV. The accompanying work of the Holy Spirit demands that it be free.
Galatians 3:1-2—"You foolish Galatians, who has bewitched you, before whose eyes Jesus Christ was publicly portrayed as crucified? This is the only thing I want to find out from you: Did you receive the Spirit by the works of the Law, or by hearing with faith?"

V. The Christian's future stability demands that it be free.

Galatians 2:20—"I have been crucified with Christ: and it is no longer I who live, but Christ lives in me; and the life which I now live in the flesh I live by faith in the Son of God, who loved me, and delivered Himself up for me."

Galatians 3:3—"Are you so foolish? Having begun by the Spirit, are you now being perfected by the flesh?"

OUTLINES THAT DEMONSTRATE REASONING FROM CAUSE TO EFFECT

The cause to effect outline uses the deductive approach. An established general premise is stated in the problem, with particular conclusions based on that premise forming the main points.

Example 1.

Scripture: Isaiah 6

Statement of Problem: What is the effect of seeing the Lord as heaven sees Him? (Isaiah 6:1-3 ". . . I saw the Lord sitting on a throne, lofty and exalted, with the train of His robe filling the temple. Seraphim stood above Him, each having six wings; . . . And one called out to another and said, 'Holy, Holy, Holy, is the Lord of hosts, the whole earth is full of His glory.' ")

I. Submission to God's work of cleansing.
Isaiah 6:5-7—"Then I said, 'Woe is me, for I am ruined! Because I am a man of unclean lips, And I live among a people of unclean lips; For my eyes have seen the King, the Lord of hosts.' Then one of the seraphim flew to me, with a burning coal in his hand which he had taken from the altar with tongs. And he touched my mouth with it and said, 'Behold, this has touched your lips; and your iniquity is taken away, and your sin is forgiven.' "

II. Obedience to God's challenge to serve. Isaiah 6:8-13.
Isaiah 6:8—"Then I heard the voice of the Lord, saying, 'Whom shall I send, and who will go for us?' Then I said, 'Here am I. Send me!' "

Example 2.

Scripture: Numbers 13, 14
Statement of Problem: What are the consequences of having the "grasshopper complex"? (The "grasshopper complex" is a concept derived from the report of the ten spies who declared, "We became like grasshoppers in our own sight, and so we were in their sight" (Numbers 13:33). Grasshoppers are known for their weakness and tendency to flee at the approach of the enemy.)

I. Walk by sight.
Chapter 13.

The spies reported seeing a land that "certainly does flow with milk and honey." (verse 27), but also that the people were "strong" and "of great size" (verse 28, 32), and "the cities are fortified and very large" (verse 28). The conclusion of those who walk by sight instead of faith is that, "We are not able to go up against the people, for they are too strong for us." (13:31).

II. Live in defeat.
Chapter 14.

A. Misery
Numbers 14:1-2 — "Then all the congregation lifted up their voice and cried, and the people wept that night. And all the sons of Israel grumbled against Moses and Aaron; and the whole congregation said to them, 'Would that we had died in the land of Egypt! Or would that we had died in this wilderness!' "

B. Rebellion
Numbers 14:9-10—" 'Only do not rebel against the Lord; and do not fear the people of the land, for they shall be our prey. Their protection has been removed from them, and the Lord is with us; do not fear them.' But all the congregation said to stone them with stones. Then the glory of the Lord appeared in the tent of meeting to all the sons of Israel."

C. Judgment
Numbers 14:34-35—"According to the number of days which you spied out the land, forty days, for every day you shall bear your guilt a year, even forty years, and you shall know My opposition. I the Lord have spoken, surely this I will do to all this evil congregation who are gathered together against Me. In this wilderness they shall be destroyed, and there they shall die."

Example 3.

Scripture: John 10
Statement of Problem: How does Christ manifest Himself as the Good Shepherd?

I. He has authority over the sheep.
John 10:1-9, 26, 27. In verses one to five He establishes His right to enter into the fold of Israel and call out those who will respond. He then leads them into the fold of salvation (10:9).

II. He meets the needs of the sheep.
John 10:9-28.

A. Life. John 10:9-11, 17, 18.
"I came that they might have life, and might have it abundantly" (10:10).

B. Food. John 10:9.
The sheep "find pasture."

C. Protection. John 10:10-14, 28.
"And I give eternal life to them; and they shall never perish, and no one shall snatch them out of My hand" (10:28).

OUTLINES THAT EMPLOY AN ANALOGY

An analogous outline stresses a similarity of attributes, effects or circumstances between objects or events. You can make this comparison throughout an outline or use a series of analogies which comprise the main points. Both of these types of outlines are illustrated below.

Example 1.

Scripture: Exodus 1-15
Statement of Problem: What are the similarities between the program whereby God delivered His people from Egyptian bondage and His present plan to bring us from death to life?

I. He encounters similar obstacles.

    A. Opposition of the world.
    6:5ff—". . . the Egyptians are holding them in bondage."

    B. Unbelief on the part of a privileged people.
    6:9—"So Moses spoke thus to the sons of Israel, but they did not listen to Moses . . ."

II. He uses a similar method of deliverance.
The Passover lamb is compared to the sacrifice of Christ on our behalf. (Compare I Corinthians 5:7).
12:12-13—"For I will go through the land of Egypt on that night, and will strike down all the first-born in the land of Egypt, both man and beast; and against all the gods of Egypt I will execute judgments—I am the Lord. And the blood shall be a sign for you on the houses where you live; and when I

see the blood I will pass over you, and no plague will befall you to destroy you when I strike the land of Egypt."

III. He receives a similar response.
   A. Some refuse and suffer the consequences.
      Exodus 12:29-30—"Now it came about at midnight that the Lord struck all the first-born in the land of Egypt, from the first-born of Pharaoh who sat on his throne to the first-born of the captive who was in the dungeon, and all the first-born of cattle. And Pharaoh arose in the night, he and all his servants and all the Egyptians; and there was a great cry in Egypt, for there was no home where there was not someone dead."

   B. Some respond and are delivered.
      Exodus 12:27—"that you shall say, 'It is a Passover sacrifice to the Lord who passed over the houses of the sons of Israel in Egypt when He smote the Egyptians, but spared our homes.' And the people bowed low and worshiped."

Example 2.

Scripture: Matthew 27:45-53
Statement of Problem: How do the three miracles at the cross help to explain the significance of the cross?

I. The darkness emphasizes the blindness of man which made the cross necessary.
   Matthew 27:45—"Now from the sixth hour darkness fell upon all the land until the ninth hour."
   Compare Amos 8:9; I John 2:8.

II. The rent veil points to the new access to God opened by the cross.
   Matthew 27:51a—"And behold the veil of the temple was torn in two from top to bottom . . ."

Compare Hebrews 10:19-22; Colossians 1:20-22; II Corinthians 3:14-18; Hebrews 9:7-8.

III. The earthquake stresses the establishment of a new foundation on the basis of the cross.
Matthew 27:51b, 52—". . . and the earth shook; and the rocks were split, and the tombs were opened; and many bodies of the saints who had fallen asleep were raised; and coming out of the tombs after His resurrection they entered the holy city and appeared to many."
Compare Hebrews 12:24-28.

OUTLINES THAT PRESENT A PATTERN

A pattern outline stresses the progressive similarities between an experience recorded in the Scripture and an experience which one might expect today. In contrast to the analogy, the actual comparisons of events are from the same category and have a recognizable affinity one to the other.

Example 1.

Scripture: Judges 13-16
Statement of Problem: In what way is Samson's life like that of many people today?

I. He was called and empowered for a great purpose.
Judges 13:25—God chose him to be separated to Himself for the purpose of delivering Israel from the Philistines.

II. He accomplished some great exploits.
Judges 14-15—He killed the lion (14:5-6), He slew 1,000 Philistines (15:11-15), He judged Israel for twenty years (15:20).

III. He lived a life of moral defeat. Judges 16.
His disobedience and compromise led to his loss of power and utter defeat.

Judges 16:20b—". . . the Lord had departed from him."

IV. He ended his life in a great manifestation of God's power.
Judges 16:28—"Then Samson called to the Lord, and said, 'O Lord God, please remember me and please strengthen me just this time, O God, that I may at once be avenged of the Philistines for my two eyes.' "

Example 2.

Scripture: II Chronicles 29-32
Statement of Problem: What kind of a revival do we need today?

I. It will have the proper preparation.
29:36b—". . . God had prepared for the people, because the thing came about suddenly."

II. It will result in a life of obedience to the Lord.
29:35b—"Thus the service of the house of the Lord was established again."
They cleansed the temple (29:3-5), offered sacrifices (29:21, 22), and "sang praises with joy, and bowed down and worshiped" (29:30).

III. It will provide for perpetuation of the experience.
The priestly ministry was restored on a continuing basis that "they might devote themselves to the law of the Lord" (31:4).

IV. It will demonstrate the depth of the experience by stedfastness in trials.
The problem was the threat from Sennacherib and the Assyrian army. The people, however, responded

91

with a confident trust in God when Hezekiah gave them the assurance that God was with them.

32:7-8—"Be strong and courageous, do not fear or be dismayed because of the king of Assyria, nor because of all the multitude which is with him; for the one with us is greater than the one with him. With him is only an arm of flesh, but with us is the Lord our God to help us and to fight our battles. And the people relied on the words of Hezekiah king of Judah."

Example 3.

Scripture: Ephesians 2:1-10
Statement of Problem: What must one understand in order to appreciate God's transforming work?

I. Recognize our desperate condition.
2:1-3—"And you were dead in your trespasses and sins, in which you formerly walked according to the course of this world, according to the prince of the power of the air, of the spirit that is now working in the sons of disobedience. Among them we too all formerly lived in the lusts of our flesh, indulging the desires of the flesh and of the mind, and were by nature children of wrath, even as the rest."

II. Recognize God's cure.
Ephesians 2:4-9.
2:8-9—"For by grace you have been saved through faith; and that not of yourselves, it is the gift of God; not as a result of works, that no one should boast."

III. Recognize God's shaping hand.
2:10—"For we are His workmanship, created in Christ Jesus for good works, which God prepared beforehand, that we should walk in them."

OUTLINES THAT
EMPHASIZE A CONTRAST

There are many opportunities available to point out differences between two doctrines, people or experiences. Law and grace, God and the devil, good and evil, Jews and Gentiles are all possibilities for development of outlines that picture a contrast.

Example 1.

Scripture: Galatians 5:16-26.
Statement of Problem: What are the respective results of yielding to the flesh and the Spirit?

I. The flesh. 19-21.
5:19—"Now the deeds of the flesh are . . ."

II. The Spirit. 22-23.
5:22—"But the fruit of the Spirit is . . ."

Example 2.

Scripture: Romans 6, 7
Statement of Problem: What are the right and wrong ways to overcome sin in our lives?

I. The wrong way. Romans 7.
This is the method of law. The law points out sin (7), but does not provide the incentive nor the power to do good (7:18).

II. The right way. Romans 6.

A. Realize our union with Christ in sharing His victory over sin. 6:1-10.

B. Consider this union a fact in every experience. 6:11.

C. Present our lives in loving obedience. 6:12-19.

Example 3.

Scripture: II Thessalonians 1
Statement of Problem: What is the contrast between the saved and unsaved?

I. In the present.

   A. Unsaved. They are in opposition to God's program. 1:4, 5.

   B. Saved. They are resting on the promises of Christ (1:1-3), enjoying the fellowship of Christians (1:3), and persevering in the service of Christ in spite of persecution (1:4).

II. In the future.

   A. Unsaved. Judgment awaits them at the revelation of Christ. 1:6-9.

   B. Saved. We will share in the glory at His coming. 1:10.

OUTLINES THAT TEACH FROM AN EXAMPLE

The main points in an outline based on an example usually consist of truths that can be learned from the experience of a Bible personality.

Example 1.

Scripture: Genesis 13, 19
Statement of Problem: What can Lot teach us?

I. About God. 19.

As Lot left the city he should have been reminded that God was:

   A. Longsuffering

   B. Just

   C. Gracious

   D. Faithful to His Word

II. About following God.

   A. Be careful of your choices. 13:10-13.

   B. Be careful that the world doesn't win your children. 19:14.

94

Example 2.

Scripture: Exodus 1-4
Statement of Problem: What can we learn from Moses
   about the methods God uses to deal with the person
   who serves Him?

I. He prepares him. 1-3.
  A. By the Pharaoh's court experience. 1.
     He gave him a background which enabled him
     to understand the Egyptians.
  B. By the backside of the desert experience. 2.
  C. By the burning bush experience. 3.
     This emphasizes the power and holiness of God.

II. He reassures him. 4:1-18.
  A. In regard to God's sufficiency. 1-9.
  B. In regard to his ability. 10-18.

Example 3.

Scripture: I Kings 17-21
Statement of Problem: What is the challenge of Elijah
   for those who would bear influence for God?

I. He had absolute faith in God's Word.
   I Kings 17:1—compare Deuteronomy 11:16, 17.
   He declared that there would be no rain. Evidently
   his contention was based on the promise in Deuteronomy that this would be God's method of judgment for unfaithfulness.

II. He had utter dependence on the power of God.
   17:4-7, 17-24. This truth is demonstrated by his
   belief that God would feed him by the ravens (17:4-
   7), and the experience of raising the widow's son
   17:17-24).

III. He was jealous that God be given the honor due His name. Chapter 18. He challenged the 450 prophets of Baal because he wanted his God to be recognized as *the* God (18:24).

IV. He needed to learn the lesson of constant dependence upon the Lord. Chapter 19. The patience of God with Elijah and His reassuring words as he sat under the juniper tree are a constant source of encouragement to all who feel the pangs of loneliness and despair.

Example 4.

Scripture: II Timothy 2:1-6
Statement of Problem: What three examples does Paul use to emphasize the importance of diligent service?

I. The soldier.
2:3-4—"Suffer hardship with me, as a good soldier of Christ Jesus. No soldier in active service entangles himself in the affairs of everyday life, so that he may please the one who enlisted him as a soldier."

II. The athlete.
2:5—"And also if any one competes as an athlete, he does not win the prize unless he competes according to the rules."

III. The farmer.
2:6—"The hard-working farmer ought to be the first to receive his share of the crops."

OUTLINES WHICH GIVE AN EXPLANATION

"Why" or "how" are the keys words in an outline which presents an explanation. The main points are designed to clarify a particular idea.

Example 1.

Scripture: Romans 8:31-39
Statement of Problem: How can we be assured of a permanent relationship of favor with God?

I. Confident repose in the work of Christ.
8:31-34—"What then shall we say to these things? If God is for us, who is against us? He who did not spare His own Son, but delivered Him up for us all, how will He not also with Him freely give us all things? Who will bring a charge against God's elect? God is the one who justifies; who is the one who condemns? Christ Jesus is He who died, yes, rather who was raised, who is at the right hand of God, who also intercedes for us."

II. Continuous triumph over the foes of the soul.
8:35, 37—"Who shall separate us from the love of Christ? Shall tribulation, or distress, or persecution, or famine, or nakedness, or peril, or sword? . . . But in all these things we overwhelmingly conquer through Him who loved us."

Example 2.

Scripture: Titus 3.
Statement of Problem: How does the Holy Spirit dethrone self and enthrone Christ?

I. Convinces us that self is falling short.
3:3—"For we also once were foolish ourselves, disobedient, deceived, enslaved to various lusts and pleasures, spending our life in malice and envy, hateful, hating one another."
This is a picture of a life without the sweetening influence of the Holy Spirit.

II. Convinces us of the need for Christ's righteousness rather than our own.
3:5, 7—"He saved us, not on the basis of deeds which we have done in righteousness, but according

to His mercy, by the washing of regeneration and renewing by the Holy Spirit, . . . that being justified by His grace we might be made heirs according to the hope of eternal life."

III. Convinces us of the need for the transforming work of the Holy Spirit.
3:5b, 6—". . . by the washing of regeneration and renewing by the Holy Spirit, whom He poured out upon us richly through Jesus Christ our Savior."

Example 3.

Scripture: Hebrews 12:3-15
Statement of Problem: Why does God discipline His children?

I. To demonstrate His love. 12:5-8.
12:6a—"For those whom the Lord loves He disciplines, . . ."

II. To produce the fruit of holiness. 9-11.
12:10b—". . . He disciplines us for our good, that we may share His holiness."

III. To encourage others by our stability. 12-15.
12:13—". . . and make straight paths for your feet, so that the limb which is lame may not be put out of joint, but rather be healed."

OUTLINES THAT STRESS INSTRUCTION

The statement of the problem of the instructive type of outline often contains such keys words as "teach," "learn" or their equivalents. Some helpful information is presented on the basis of a scriptural incident or idea.

Example 1.

Scripture: I John 2:1-2
Statement of Problem: What do we learn from John as to the proper attitude toward sin in the life of the believer?

I. God has revealed the instructions whereby we need not sin.
2:1a—"My little children, I am writing these things to you that you may not sin."

II. We are in constant danger of sinning.
2:1b—"And if anyone sins, . . ."

III. God has made provisions for restoration when we do sin.
2:1c, 2a—". . . we have an Advocate with the Father, Jesus Christ the righteous; and He Himself is the propitiation for our sins; . . ."

Example 2.

Scripture: I Corinthians 11:17-34
Statement of Problem: What does the Lord want us to remember at communion?

I. The price of our redemption.
11:24, 25—"And when He had given thanks, He broke it, and said, 'This is My body which is for you; do this in remembrance of Me.' In the same way the cup also, after supper, saying 'This cup is the new covenant in My blood; do this, as often as you drink it, in remembrance of Me.' "

II. The basis of fellowship at the Lord's Supper.
11:18, 20, 21, 29—"For, in the first place, when you come together as a church, I hear that divisions exist among you; and in part, I believe it. . . . Therefore when you meet together, it is not to eat the Lord's Supper, for in your eating each one takes his own supper first; and one is hungry and another is drunk. . . . For he who eats and drinks, eats and drinks judgment to himself, if he does not judge the body rightly."

III. The beginning of the new covenant.
11:25-26—"In the same way the cup also, after supper, saying, 'This cup is the new covenant in My

blood; do this, as often as you drink it, in remembrance of Me.' For as often as you eat this bread and drink the cup, you proclaim the Lord's death until He comes."

Example 3.

Scripture: II Corinthians 12:7-10
Statement of Problem: What does God desire to teach us about the purpose of difficult circumstances?

I. To be receptive to His grace.
12:9a—"And He has said to me, 'My grace is sufficient for you,' . . ."

II. To be dependent on His power.
12:9b—". . . power is perfected in weakness."

III. To be content with His provision.
12:10—"Therefore I am well content with weaknesses, with insults, with distresses, with persecutions, with difficulties, for Christ's sake; for when I am weak, then I am strong."

OUTLINES WHOSE MAIN POINTS ARE COMPONENT PARTS OF A WHOLE

When the sum of the main points added together approximate the statement of the problem this is described as an outline wherein the ideas are component parts of the total concept.

Example 1.

Scripture: Deuteronomy 6:4-12
Statement of Problem: What are the essentials for establishing a home with a solid foundation?

I. A heart love for the Lord.
6:5-6—"And you shall love the Lord your God with all your heart and with all your soul and with all your might. And these words, which I am commanding you today, shall be on your heart."

II. A willingness to instruct the children in the Word of the Lord.

6:7-9—"and you shall teach them diligently to your sons and shall talk of them when you sit in your house and when you walk by the way and when you lie down and when you rise up. And you shall bind them as a sign on your hand and they shall be as frontals on your forehead. And you shall write them on the doorposts of your house and on your gates."

III. A constant expression of thanksgiving for His provision.

6:10-12—"Then it shall come about when the Lord your God brings you into the land which He swore to your fathers, Abraham, Isaac and Jacob, to give you, great and splendid cities, which you did not build, and houses full of all good things which you did not fill, and hewn cisterns which you did not dig, vineyards and olive trees, which you did not plant, and you shall eat and be satisfied then watch yourself lest you forget the Lord who brought you from the land of Egypt, out of the house of slavery."

Apply each of the ingredients of the component parts of the outline and you will be assured of a "home with a solid foundation."

Example 2.

Scripture: Matthew 3:3-12
Statement of Problem: What was the message of John the Baptist?

I. A reminder of coming judgment.

3:7, 10—"But when he saw many of the Pharisees and Sadducees coming for baptism, he said to them, 'You brood of vipers, who warned you to flee from the wrath to come? . . . And the axe is already laid at the root of the trees; every tree therefore that does not bear good fruit is cut down, and thrown into the fire.' "

II. A plea to examine the basis of deliverance.
3:8, 9, 11, 12—"Therefore bring forth fruit in keeping with your repentance; and do not suppose that you can say to yourselves, 'We have Abraham for our father,' for I say unto you, that God is able from these stones to raise up children to Abraham. . . . As for me, I baptize you in water for repentance; but He who is coming after me is mightier than I, and I am not even fit to remove His sandals; He Himself will baptize you with the Holy Spirit and fire. And His winnowing fork is in His hand, and He will thoroughly clean His threshing-floor; and He will gather His wheat into the barn, but He will burn up the chaff with unquenchable fire."
He challenges them to turn from dependence on Abraham to a recognition of Christ.

Example 3.

Scripture: Acts 4, 5
Statement of Problem: How is the New Testament church characterized?

I. Love.

A. For souls
5:42—"And every day, in the temple and from house to house, they kept right on teaching and preaching Jesus as the Christ."

B. For one another
4:32—"And the congregation of those who bebelieved were of one heart and soul; and not one of them claimed that anything belonging to him was his own; but all things were common property to them."

II. Exclusiveness.

A. In message
4:12—"And there is salvation in no one else; for there is no other name under heaven that has

been given among men, by which we must be saved."

   B. In membership
    Chapter 5—Ananias and Sapphira were permanently excluded from membership because of hypocrisy!

III. Opposition.
   5:40—"And they took his advice; and after calling the apostles in, they flogged them and ordered them to speak no more in the name of Jesus, and then released them."

IV. Power.
   4:31, 33—"And when they had prayed, the place where they had gathered together was shaken, and they were all filled with the Holy Spirit, and began to speak the word of God with boldness. . . . And with great power the apostles were giving witness to the resurrection of the Lord Jesus, and abundant grace was upon them all."

OUTLINES WHICH
ESTABLISH CONDITIONS

In some outlines the main points establish the conditions for accomplishing a work or having an experience. The word "if" is either stated or implied in the "statement of problem."

Example 1.

Scripture: Colossians 2:1-19
Statement of Problem: What is necessary if one is to be complete in Christ? (Colossians 2:10)

I. Accept His righteousness.
   2:13-14—"And when you were dead in your transgressions and the uncircumcision of your flesh, He made you alive together with Him, having forgiven us all our transgressions, having cancelled out the

certificate of debt consisting of decrees against us and which was hostile to us; and He has taken it out of the way, having nailed it to the cross."

II. Recognize His knowledge.
2:3—"In whom are hidden all the treasures of wisdom and knowledge."

III. Submit to His direction.
2:19—"And not holding fast to the Head, from whom the entire body, being supplied and held together by the joints and ligaments, grows with a growth which is from God."

Example 2.

Scripture: I Thessalonians 1
Statement of Problem: What must one realize if he is to be an effective witness for Christ?

I. How to live.
1:5b, 6—". . . you know what kind of men we proved to be among you for your sake. You also became imitators of us and of the Lord, having received the word in much tribulation with the joy of the Holy Spirit."

II. What power is available.
1:5a—"For our gospel did not come to you in word only, but also in power and in the Holy Spirit and with full conviction; . . ."

III. What to say.
1:5a—"For our gospel . . ."
1:8a—"For the word of the Lord has sounded forth from you, . . ."

IV. What to expect. 6-10.
A. Tribulation
1:6b—". . . much tribulation. . ."
B. Joy
1:6c—". . . with the joy of the Holy Spirit."

C. Transformed lives
1:9—"For they themselves report about us what kind of a reception we had with you, and how you turned to God from idols to serve a living and true God."

OUTLINES THAT CHALLENGE ONE TO ACCEPT RESPONSIBILITY

In this type of outline the main points indicate a challenge to action based on the statement of the problem.

Example 1.

Scripture: II Peter 3:14-18
Statement of Problem: What should be our response to the expectation of Christ's coming?

I. Make certain of our salvation.
3:15—"And regard the patience of our Lord to be salvation; just as also our beloved brother Paul, according to the wisdom given him, wrote to you."

II. Purpose to please Christ.
3:14—"Therefore, beloved, since you look for these things, be diligent to be found by Him in peace, spotless and blameless."

III. Dedicate ourselves to the truth of Christ.
3:16, 17—"As also in all his letters, speaking in them of these things, in which are some things hard to understand, which the untaught and unstable distort, as they do also the rest of the Scriptures, to their own destruction. You therefore, beloved, knowing this beforehand, be on your guard lest, being carried away by the error of unprincipled men, you fall from your own steadfastness."

IV. Set our goal on growth in Christ.
3:18—"But grow in the grace and knowledge of our Lord and Savior Jesus Christ. To Him be the glory, both now and to the day of eternity. Amen."

Example 2.

Scripture: Colossians 3:1-5
Statement of Problem: What should be our response to having been raised with Christ?

I. Set our minds on things above.
3:1, 2—"If then you have been raised up with Christ, keep seeking the things above, where Christ is, seated at the right hand of God. Set your mind on the things above, not on the things that are on earth."

II. Express our deadness to the things of earth.
3:3-5—"For you have died and your life is hidden with Christ in God. When Christ, who is our life, is revealed, then you also will be revealed with Him in glory. Therefore consider the members of your earthly body as dead to immorality, impurity, passion, evil desire, and greed, which amounts to idolatry."

OUTLINES WHOSE MAIN POINTS EMBODY INTERROGATION

An outline in which the main points are stated in question form is known as an interrogation type.

Example 1.

Scripture: Romans 14
Statement of Problem: What five questions will help us determine if an action is right?

I. Will it bring glory to God? 14:6-8.

14:8—"For if we live, we live for the Lord, or if we die, we die for the Lord; therefore whether we live or die, we are the Lord's."

II. Does it emphasize that which is most important?

14:17-18—"For the kingdom of God is not eating and drinking, but righteousness and peace and joy in the Holy Spirit. For he who in this way serves Christ is acceptable to God and approved by men."

It should be pointed out that there will be eating and drinking in the kingdom (compare Matthew 26:29), but they are not the most important activities.

III. Will it build up my brother?

14:13, 19—"Therefore let us not judge one another any more, but rather determine this—not to put an obstacle or a stumbling-block in a brother's way. . . . So then let us pursue the things which make for peace and the building up of one another."

IV. Do I feel right about it?

14:22, 23—"The faith which you have, have as your own conviction before God. Happy is he who does not condemn himself in what he approves. But he who doubts is condemned if he eats, because his eating is not from faith; and whatever is not from faith is sin."

V. Would I be pleased to have it brought into the open at the judgment of Christ?

14:10b, 12—"For we shall all stand before the judgment-seat of God. . . . So then each one of us shall give account of himself to God."

Example 2.

Scripture: Revelation 3:14, 20

Statement of Problem: What questions must be answered before we will be impressed with Christ's final admonition to the church?

107

I. To whom is it addressed?
He is evidently standing at the door of the individual members of the church of Laodicea. (see verse 14)

II. Who is speaking?
3:14b—". . . The Amen, the faithful and true Witness, the Beginning of the creation of God, says this."

III. What is his offer?
3:20c—". . . I will come in to him, and will dine with him, and he with Me."

IV. What are the conditions for accepting the offer?
3:20b—". . . if any one hears My voice and opens the door, . . ."

OUTLINES WHOSE MAIN POINTS MOVE IN A TIME SEQUENCE

The main points of a time sequence outline are based on a movement of time, usually involving some arrangement of past, present and future.

Example 1.

Scripture: Deuteronomy 8
Statement of Problem: Why did God encourage Israel to stop and think?

I. That they might profit from past experiences. 8:2, 3.
8:2a—"And you shall remember all the way which the Lord your God has led you in the wilderness . . ."

II. That they might stress what is important in the present.
8:6—"Therefore, you shall keep the commandments of the Lord your God, to walk in His ways and to fear Him."

III. That they might anticipate the future in the light of the power of God. 8:7-20.
8:16b—". . . that He might humble you and that He might test you, to do good for you in the end."

Example 2.

Scripture: Ephesians 5:25b-27
Statement of Problem: What is the progress of Christ's work on behalf of the church?

I. In the past, He gave Himself for her.
5:25b—". . . Christ also loved the church and gave Himself up for her."

II. In the present, He is sanctifying her.
5:26—"that He might sanctify her, having cleansed her by the washing of water with the word."

III. In the future, He will present her to Himself.
5:27—"that He might present to Himself the church in all her glory, having no spot or wrinkle or any such thing; but that she should be holy and blameless."

OUTLINES THAT DESCRIBE SOMETHING

In a description type of outline the main points describe various facets of a scene or an event.

Example.

Scripture: Revelation 22:1-5
Statement of Problem: What three scenes are portrayed by John as he describes the future home of the saints?

I. The river.

22:1, 2a—"And he showed me a river of the water of life, clear as crystal, coming from the throne of God and of the Lamb, in the middle of its street."

II. The tree of life.

22:2b—". . . on either side of the river was the tree of life, . . ."

III. The throne of God.

22:3-5—"And there shall no longer be any curse; and the throne of God and of the Lamb shall be in it, and His bond-servants shall serve Him; and they shall see His face, and His name shall be on their foreheads. And there shall no longer be any night; and they shall not have need of the light of a lamp nor the light of the sun, because the Lord God shall illumine them; and they shall reign forever and ever."

THE
PREACHING PROGRAM

THE PREACHING PROGRAM

Essential to the success of any pulpit ministry is careful advance planning. Every pastor who has been faced with week to week sermon preparation can sympathize with the pastor who reclined in his easy chair after a busy Sunday, held his head in his hands and sighed, "Two more next week!" A general outline of a preaching program for the months ahead eases the pressure of always preparing for an immediate deadline.

Thoughtful consideration of your preaching program also enables you to present a balanced ministry of the Word. When you must scramble weekly for a text to preach on it is easy to neglect many portions of Scripture. The temptation is to concentrate on the more familiar and the most easily developed texts. But remember, faithfulness to the Word obligates you to preach the whole counsel of God.

ADVANCE PLANNING

Many ministers find it helpful to plan their preaching at least a year in advance. Summer vacation time provides an opportunity to consider objectively where you have been and where you are going. After careful evaluation, choose your sermon themes for the year ahead according to the needs of your people and the subject material most appropriate in presenting the full orbit of God's truth.

List the sermons according to the date on which each is to be preached, the theme, and the purpose you want to accomplish. This will help you accumulate ideas for the sermons, especially appropriate quotations and illustrations. Establish a system for storing the material you have gleaned. This will give you a storehouse of ideas already in hand when the time for actual written preparation begins.

TYPES OF SERIES

Some suggestions for types of series are:

1. **Exposition of books of the Bible.**
   Probably the most common series of sermons is the one taken from a Bible book. A paragraphed Bible helps you identify changes of thought on the part of the Bible writer. Divide your messages according to these paragraphs making an effort to discover the thrust of each. This thrust provides the clue to the problem to be solved in the development of the sermon.

   It is helpful at times to present messages from a book based on a general outline of that book. Each point in the outline becomes the unifying thought of a sermon. For example, the Book of Romans lends itself to six themes.

   1) Condemnation 1-3:8

   2) Justification 3:9-5:21

   3) Sanctification 6, 7

   4) Glorification 8

   5) Clarification 9-11 (In regard to Israel)

   6) Application 12-16

   At a later date the same book can be divided by chapters or paragraphs. In this way you can preach on the same book, develop new ideas from a different perspective, and thus enhance understanding of the Word.

2. **Through the Bible series.**
   A "Through the Bible" series forces you to cover the entire Bible in your preaching. Some ministers proceed from Genesis to Revelation over a period of several years. You may wish to preach this series either in the morning or evening and leave the alternate sermon for a variety of subject matters. There is a tendency for monotony to result when you preach exclusively from either the Old

or New Testament over a long period. To overcome this danger, alternate Old and New Testament books.

Some ministers treat an entire book in one sermon making a total of 66 messages. The usual method, however, is to pick out the high points of a book that best presents the overall message intended. Each of these points of emphasis form the basis of a message. For example, in the Book of Genesis the sermons could be based on personalities such as Adam, Noah, Abraham, Isaac, Jacob and Joseph. Another possibility is to emphasize events such as creation, the fall, the flood, the confusion of tongues, the choosing of Abraham, etc.

When you begin a through the Bible series remember that completing such a program will require an extended period of time. It will also require much diligent research in books that probably have been previously neglected.

3. Doctrinal.

A different approach to preaching is provided by the development of doctrinal series. Possibilities for such a series include the great doctrines of the faith, or the treatment of individual subjects such as the attributes of God, the Church or the Holy Spirit. The task of the preacher is to relate the most meaningful passages of Scripture to the subject.

4. Practical.

All preaching requires practical application, but there is a place for the development of a series of messages dealing with practical matters such as the relationships within the home. Some ministers set aside an extended period to preaching on this vital subject. Another possibility would be the treatment of the Christian attitude toward human government, war, race, labor and other current topics of debate.

THE USE OF THE CALENDAR

In your preaching program, take advantage of interest generated by holiday publicity, especially that surrounding the religious holidays. Usually very little is lost by interrupting a series already in progress in order to emphasize a seasonal theme. It is surprising, however, how often a series can be adjusted to include the seasonal emphasis and sometimes provide the climax to a group of messages. For example, if you are preaching through one of the gospels, the ideal time to reach the final chapters would be prior to Easter, with the resurrection and ascension fitting into their proper places according to the Christian year.

The following suggestions relate to specific days:

1. New Year's Day.

While not specifically designated as a religious holiday, New Year's Day has definite religious implications. It affords an opportunity to emphasize a new start, the urgency of the hour, and the necessity to buy up opportunities. Many Bible personalities provide a basis for stressing the foregoing. Among them are Moses, Samson, Jonah, Peter and the Prodigal Son.

2. Easter.

Both pre-Easter and post-Easter series have potential for effective challenge. Pre-Easter possibilities are the personalities at the cross, miracles from the triumphal entry to the resurrection and the famous seven last words of Christ.

Following Easter you can stress the commands of Christ after the resurrection such as "wait," "go," "follow," "teach," "feed," "love," "tend," and "baptize."

3. Mother's Day.

Mother's Day provides occasion for instruction in the establishment of the Christian home. Avoid simple eulogies of mothers. Passages of Scripture which are appropriate for this occasion are: II John which is a letter from John to a mother; John 19: 26, 27 where Christ instructs as to the care of His mother; and II Timothy 1:1-14 which stresses the part that Timothy's mother and grandmother had in training him.

4. Thanksgiving.

The celebration of Thanksgiving has deteriorated to the point where the original purpose has been largely forgotten. Christians need to be reminded that the Bible has much to say about the response of thanksgiving for all God has done for us. Examples of verses that stress this are Ephesians 3:13-21, Romans 12:1, 2 and Luke 17:11-19.

5. Christmas.

The increasing commercialization of Christmas makes it imperative that the true meaning of Christ's entrance into the world be proclaimed by the church. Why not preach a sermon on keeping Christ in Christmas on the first Sunday after Thanksgiving. In some areas this may coincide with the annual arrival of Santa Claus to the shopping centers and the installation of Christmas decorations.

Chapter VI

IMPROVING DELIVERY

IMPROVING DELIVERY

The musician is known for his dedication to improving the quality of his performance. Most professional singers must spend hours perfecting intricate techniques. Yet the minister, who should have an even greater desire to make his message appealing, often does relatively nothing to develop his skill in delivery. If you would like to change this pattern and set up higher goals for your preaching, the following suggestions will be of help.

1. Be excited about your message.

Probably the most common fault of preachers is apathy. Unless you are thrilled with the message, it is presumptuous to expect your audience to be. Of course, you must discover ideas that are worthy of excitement. Many common truths, however, can be given new urgency if you constantly seek the guidance of the Holy Spirit who illuminates the life-giving message.

2. Speak in a conversational manner, but with intensity.

A minister may be very communicative when talking to one or two people, but become a different person in the pulpit. Some actually try to imitate a speaker with whom they have become enamored. An affected forcefulness is sometimes substituted for meaningful communication. Others fall into the pattern of a high-pitched whine known as the "holy tone." If preaching is to be effective, the listener must feel that the minister is speaking directly to him as an individual. A conversational manner is not to be equated with a casual manner. Conversations are often characterized by a high degree of intensity. This should be the goal of the preacher.

3. Think communication.

Ask yourself constantly, "Is the audience grasping what I have to say?" Many think only about the material and the choice of words by which it is communicated. Master the ideas so that you can concentrate on imparting them. Develop a system of sermon notes which will allow you the most freedom to think about the delivery of your message.

4. Look your listeners directly in the eye.

Talking to a person who is unable to look you in the eye is very disconcerting. An audience responds in the same way to a speaker who fails to establish eye contact. When you look at the rear wall, or just above the eyes of the listener, you appear evasive and insincere. You must have direct contact with the *eyes* of individuals. However, be careful not to concentrate your attention on the same people, or look at any one person so long that he becomes uncomfortable. You do not need to look at everyone. When an individual in an audience observes you establishing eye contact with others, he will give you credit as though you were looking directly at him.

To help yourself establish better eye contact, write the sermon notes in your Bible beside the passage you are expounding. This will enable you to look at the Scripture, check your notes, and then look at the audience. This eliminates the necessity for looking at notes on the pulpit to remind you of the next idea.

5. Develop audience awareness.

The response of listeners is constantly changing. By the expression on their faces, the alert speaker can detect antagonism, disagreement, and waning interest. Recognize these reactions, then adjust the content of your message, as well as your delivery, accordingly.

6. Use inflection to advantage.

Inflection is the modulation or change of pitch within a word. You can enhance the depth of meaning of your words by increasing the changes in pitch. For example, say the word "no" first starting from a low pitch and then sliding to a high pitch. Now, reverse the procedure. The possible variations in meaning through the use of inflection are innumerable. Listen to recordings of effective speakers and imitate their inflections.

7. Cultivate the use of the pause.

Most speakers seem to fear quietness. They tend to fill any blank spaces with meaningless words, or a "ministerial grunt." However, listen to many of the better speakers, and you will discover that they often pause at the appropriate time. The pauses give the audience a chance to digest what has been said, and provide opportunity for the speaker to judge response.

8. Improve your voice quality.

The tape recorder is an invaluable aid to the speaker who desires to improve his voice quality, including problems of audibility, resonance, articulation, and general unpleasantness. Listen to a recording of your message. If you detect a serious problem, seek the advice of a speech expert who can recommend proper voice exercises to help you overcome the difficulty.

9. Be natural in your gestures and bodily movements.

Facial expressions, gestures, and bodily movements are indicators of a speaker's confidence. Your goal is to appear relaxed. This puts the audience at ease and permits them to concentrate fully on the speaker's message. If you are plagued by stage fright to the point where natural movement is difficult, remind yourself with the Apostle Paul that

"... We do not preach *ourselves* but Christ Jesus as Lord ..." (II Corinthians 4:5).

The video tape recorder is a useful tool to help you see yourself as others see you. It permits you to objectively analyze all of your movements, seeking to improve those where the correction is needed.

Some seminaries are now offering summer refresher courses for active ministers to enable them to obtain exposure to a video tape recorder.

10. Listen to the criticism of others.

Too often preachers tend to count criticism of their sermons as a personal affront to their calling as a divine spokesman. On the contrary, ministers need to encourage the critical analysis of their sermons. Some pastors prefer to have their wives act in this capacity. Others seek the counsel of members of the congregation. The wise preacher will recognize his constant need for improvement in sermon delivery, and work with eternal diligence to remedy the faults.

BIBLIOGRAPHY

BIBLIOGRAPHY

Arndt, William F. and Gingrich, F. Wilbur (eds.). *A Greek English Lexicon of the New Testament and Other Early Christian Literature.* Chicago: The University of Chicago Press, 1957.

Barnhouse, Donald Grey. *Let Me Illustrate.* Westwood, N.J.: F. H. Revell Company, 1967.

Bartlett, Gene E. *The Audacity of Preaching.* New York: Harper & Bros., 1962.

Broadus, John A. *The Preparation and Delivery of Sermons.* Weatherspoon Edition. New York: Harper & Bros., 1944.

Blackwood, Andrew W. *Biographical Preaching for Today.* New York: Abingdon Press, 1954.

.... *Doctrinal Preaching for Today.* New York: Abingdon Press, 1956.

.... *The Fine Art of Preaching.* New York: The Macmillan Co., 1937.

.... *Planning a Years Pulpit Work.* New York: Abingdon Press, 1942.

.... *Preaching from the Bible.* New York: Abingdon Press, 1941.

.... *The Preparation of Sermons.* New York: Abingdon Press, 1948.

Caemmerer, Richard R. *Preaching for the Church.* St. Louis: Concordia Publishing House, 1959.

Clowney, Edmund. *Preaching and Biblical Theology.* Grand Rapids: Eerdmans Publishing House, 1961.

Cohen, Abraham. *Jewish Homiletics.* London: M. L. Cailingold, 1937.

Cook, Thomas. *Soul-Saving Preaching.* London: Charles H. Kelly, n.d.

Dalton, Arthur E. *Brief and to the Point: Suggestions for Preachers.* London: James Clarke and Co., 1961.

Davidson, B. *The Hebrew Analytical and Chaldee Lexicon.* London: Samuel Bagster and Sons Ltd.

Davis, H. Grady. *Design for Preaching.* Philadelphia: Muhlenberg Press, 1958.

Gammie, Alexander. *Preachers I Have Heard.* London: Pickering and Inglis Ltd., 1945.

Jackson, Benjamin Franklin, ed. *Audio-Visual Facilities and Equipment for Churchmen.* Nashville: Abingdon Press, 1969.

.... *Creative Communication Skills for Churchmen.* Nashville: Abingdon Press, 1970.

.... *Television, Radio, Films for Churchmen.* Nashville: Abingdon Press, 1969.

Jackson, Edgar. *How to Preach to People's Needs.* New York: Abingdon Press, 1956.

.... *A Psychology for Preaching.* New York: Channel Press, 1961.

Kemp, Charles F. *The Preaching Pastor.* St. Louis: Bethany Press, 1966.

Killinger, J. *The Centrality of Preaching in the Total Task of the Ministry.* Waco, Texas: Word Books, 1969.

Kittel, G. (ed). *Theological Dictionary of the New Testament.* 8 volumes when completed. Grand Rapids: Eerdmans Publishing House, 1964.

Koller, Charles W. *Expository Preaching Without Notes.* Grand Rapids: Baker Book House, 1962.

Lenski, Richard C. H. *The Sermon: Its Homiletical Construction.* Grand Rapids: Baker Book House, 1968. (reprint of 1927 edition).

Lewis, Ralph L. *Speech for Persuasive Preaching.* Wilmore, Kentucky: Asbury Theological Seminary, 1968.

Littorin, Frank. *How to Preach the Word with Variety.* Grand Rapids: Baker Book House, 1953.

Macartney, Clarence Edward. *Preaching Without Notes.* New York: Abingdon Press, 1943.

McLaughlin, Raymond. *Communication for the Church.* Zondervan Publishing House, 1968.

McCleod, Donald. *Here is My Method: The Art of Sermon Construction.* Westwood, N.J.: F. H. Revell Co., 1952.

Meyer, F. B. *Jottings and Hints for Lay Preachers.* London: Andrew Melrose, 1903.

.... *Expository Preaching Plans and Methods.* New York: Doran Press, 1910.

Miller, Donald G. *The Way to Biblical Preaching.* Nashville: Abingdon Press, 1957.

Moorehead, Lee. *Freedom of the Pulpit.* New York: Abingdon Press, 1961.

Morgan, G. Campbell. *The Ministry of the Word.* New York: Fleming H. Revell Co., 1919.

O'Neal, Glenn. *An Analytical Study of Certain Rhetorical Factors Used by Billy Graham in the 1949 Los Angeles Meetings.* Unpublished doctoral dissertation, The University of Southern California, Los Angeles, 1956.

Perry, Lloyd M. *Biblical Sermon Guide*. Grand Rapids: Baker Book House, 1970.

Perry, Lloyd M. and Whitesell, Faris D. *Variety in Your Preaching*. Westwood, N.J.: F. H. Revell Co., 1954.

Reu, J. M. *Homiletics*. Grand Rapids: Baker Book House, 1967. (reprint of 1924 edition).

Robinson, James H. *Adventurous Preaching*. Great Neck, New York: Channel Press, 1956.

Roddy, Clarence. *We Prepare and Preach*. Chicago: Moody Press, 1959.

Sangster, William E. *The Craft of Sermon Construction*. Philadelphia: Westminster Press, 1951.

Stevenson, Dwight E. *In the Biblical Preacher's Workshop*. Nashville: Abingdon Press, 1967.

Stewart, James S. *Preaching*. London: Hodder and Stoughton, 1955.

Stott, John R. W. *The Preacher's Portrait*. Grand Rapids: Eerdmans Publishing House, 1961.

Tizard, Leslie J. *Preaching: The Art of Communication*. New York: Oxford University Press, 1959.

Toombs, Lawrence E. *The Old Testament in Christian Preaching*. Philadelphia: Westminster Press, 1961.

Turnbull, Ralph (ed.). *Baker's Dictionary of Practical Theology*. Grand Rapids: Baker Book House, 1967.

Unger, Merrill F. *Principles of Expository Preaching*. Grand Rapids: Zondervan Publishing House, 1955.

Vine, W. F. *Expository Dictionary of New Testament Words*. London: Oliphants Ltd., 1952.

White, Douglas M. *He Expounded: A Guide to Expository Preaching*. Chicago: Moody Press, 1952.

Yohn, David Waite. *The Contemporary Preacher and His Task*. Grand Rapids: Eerdmans Publishing House, 1969.

APPENDIX

APPENDIX

1. WORK SHEET FOR
INITIAL SERMON PREPARATION

Scripture:

1. Historical and Biblical Background.

2. Exegetical meaning of passage:

    a. paraphrase

    b. usage of words in other contexts

    c. variations of text in other versions

3. Emotional meaning of passage.

4. Inferences.

5. Related texts.

6. Wrong ideas corrected by text.

7. Illustrations.

2. WORK SHEET FOR ORGANIZATION OF A SERMON

Main thrust of passage.

Relation to needs of audience.

Statement of problem.

Outline (ideas arranged from sermon preparation work sheet)

    I.

        A.

        B.

           1.

           2.

    II.

Introduction
Background material

Method of arousing interest

Conclusion
Review

Specific action suggested

3. WORK SHEET FOR ANALYSIS OF A SERMON

NOTE: Your speaking is rated according to the following scale: 5—Superior; 4—Good; 3—Average; 2—Poor; 1—Inadequate.

Student ....

Course .... Date ....

I
USE OF THE VOICE ☐

Audibility	Rate	Pitch	Authoritativeness
Inaudible	Too slow	Too high	Lacking
Well adapted	Appropriate	Pleasant	Impressive
Too loud	Too fast	Too low	Overbearing

Suggestions:

II
BODILY ACTION ☐

Posture	Movement	Gestures
Too informal	Too little	Too few
Good poise	Purposeful	Natural
Too rigid	Random	Excessive

Eye Contact		Facial Expression
Lacking		Lacking
Personal		Consistent
Too individual		Too severe

Suggestions:

III
DICTION AND USAGE ☐

Language	Sentences	Vocabulary	Pronunciation
Too simple	Too short	Too meager	Careless
Striking	Well formed	Good choice	Correct
Flowery	Too long	Too scholarly	Pedantic

Suggestions:

IV
SPEECH DEVELOPMENT

Introduction ☐   **Outline** ☐   **Ideas** ☐   **Conclusion** ☐

Attention Favorable Lacking	**Proposition** Indefinite Clear	**Source** Biblical Non-biblical	**Purpose** Lacking Direct tie-up

Arousal of Interest **in Subject** Vital Lacking	**Main Ideas** Indistinct Clear	**Interpretation** Correct Faulty	**Presentation** Stirred to action Weak

Background **Material** Sufficient Lacking	**Transitions** Smooth Clumsy	**Worthiness** Vital Lacking	**Length** Too long Appropriate Too short

Length
Too long
Appropriate
Too short

Illustrations
Lacking
Appropriate

Suggestions:

V
SPEAKER-AUDIENCE RELATION ☐

Speaker's Appearance
Timid
Respectful
Overbearing

Speaker's Attitude
Lacking sincerity
Vitally concerned

Audience Reaction
Inattentive
Interested
Hostile

Speaker's Directness
Lacking
Conversational
Too intimate

TOTAL SCORE:
